100% Job Search
SUCCESS

100% Job Search SUCCESS

AMY SOLOMON, MS, OTR

LORI TYLER, MS

TERRY TAYLOR, PhD

WADSWORTH
CENGAGE Learning™

Australia • Brazil • Japan • Korea • Mexico • Singapore • Spain • United Kingdom • United States

100% Job Search Success
Amy Solomon, MS, OTR • Lori Tyler, MS •
Terry Taylor, PhD

Vice President, Career Education SBU:
Dawn Gerrain

Director of Learning Solutions:
Sherry Dickinson

Managing Editor: Robert L. Serenka, Jr.

Acquisitions Editor: Martine Edwards

Product Manager: Jennifer Anderson

Editorial Assistant: Falon Ferraro

Director of Production: Wendy A. Troeger

Production Manager: J.P. Henkel

Content Project Manager: Amber Leith

Technology Project Manager:
Sandy Charette

Director of Marketing: Wendy E. Mapstone

Channel Manager: Gerard McAvey

Marketing Coordinator: Jonathan Sheehan

Cover and Text Design: Suzanne Nelson,
essence of 7

For product information and technology assistance, contact us
at **Cengage Learning Customer & Sales Support, 1-800-354-9706**.

For permission to use material from this text or product,
submit all requests online at **www.cengage.com/permissions**.
Further permissions questions can be emailed to
permissionrequest@cengage.com.

Library of Congress Control Number: 2006019205

ISBN-13: 978-1-4180-1631-9
ISBN-10: 1-4180-1631-4

Wadsworth
10 Davis Drive
Belmont, CA 94002-3098
USA

Cengage Learning is a leading provider of customized learning solutions with office locations around the globe, including Singapore, the United Kingdom, Australia, Mexico, Brazil, and Japan. Locate your local office at: **www.cengage.com/global**

Cengage Learning products are represented in Canada by Nelson Education, Ltd.

To learn more about Wadsworth, visit **www.cengage.com/Wadsworth**

Purchase any of our products at your local college store or at our preferred online store
www.ichapters.com

NOTICE TO THE READER

Printed in China by China Translation & Printing Services Limited
6 7 8 9 12 11 10

Contents

Preface / xiv

Acknowledgments / xx

1 INDUSTRY AND JOB RESEARCH **3**

Understanding Your Industry and Your Place within It / 4
>   *Your Interests / 4*
>   *Your Abilities / 5*
>   *Your Values / 5*
>   *Your Personality / 6*
>   *Industry Requirements / 6*
>   *Professional Culture / 8*

Professional Socialization / 11

Sources for Industry Research / 13
>   *The Internet / 13*
>   *Government Sources / 14*
>   *Professional Organizations / 14*
>   *Networking / 15*
>   *Informational Interviews / 15*
>   *Faculty / 16*
>   *Career Services / 16*
>   *Professional Job Counselors / 16*
>   *Libraries / 17*

Staying Current and Updated / 17
>   *Professional Organizations / 17*
>   *Professional Publications / 18*

Continuing Education and Conferences / 18
Certification and Licensure Boards / 18
Electronic Communication / 19

2 ASSESSING AND DEVELOPING SKILLS FOR THE WORKPLACE 25

Setting Goals for Your Professional Pursuit / 26

Know Yourself / 28
Self-Assessment Tools / 28

Gaining Experience: The Overview / 30

The Internship / 31
Purpose of an Internship / 31
Locating the Best Internship / 33
Internship Success / 35

3 DEVELOPING A PROFESSIONAL PORTFOLIO 43

Purposes of Professional Portfolios / 44
Marketing Your Skills in Job Interviews / 45
Documenting Professional Development Activities / 45
Guiding Your Professional Development / 45
Supporting Requests for Salary Increases or Promotions / 46
Qualifying for Bonuses and Other Financial Awards / 46

Types of Portfolios / 46
The Learning or Developmental Portfolio / 46
The Assessment Portfolio / 47
The Professional or Career Portfolio / 47

Portfolio Formats / 49
Electronic Formats / 49
Hard Copy Portfolios / 50
Combination Portfolios / 50

Contents of the Portfolio / 50

Selecting Artifacts / 51
The Professional or Career Portfolio / 51
The Learning or Developmental Portfolio / 52
The Assessment Portfolio / 52

Organizing the Portfolio / 54
Functional Organization / 54
Chronological Organization / 55

Evaluating the Portfolio / 55

4 NETWORKING AND SELF-PROMOTION. 61

What Is Networking? / 62
What Networking Is Not / 63
What Networking Is / 64
The Purpose of Networking / 65

Networking Venues / 65
Existing Networks / 65
Created Networks / 66

Steps in the Networking Process / 67
Maximizing Your Networking Success / 70

Other Networking Techniques / 73
The Elevator Speech / 73
The Informational Interview / 75

5 RESUME AND COVER LETTER DEVELOPMENT 83

Purpose of the Resume / 84

Types of Resumes / 85
The Chronological Resume / 85
The Functional Resume / 86

Combination Resumes / 88
The Curriculum Vitae / 89

Resume Formats / 89
  Electronic Resumes / 89
  Web Resumes / 90
  Selecting a Resume Format / 90

Guidelines to Creating a Resume / 90

Utilizing Technology to Send Resumes / 94
  Sending Resumes via E-Mail / 94
  Posting Resumes on the Web / 95
  Safety on the Web / 96

Cover Letters / 97
  Other Types of Correspondence / 99

References and Recommendations / 99

6   DRESSING FOR SUCCESS 107

First Impressions / 109

Dressing for Success / 110
  Body Type / 110

Dressing for the Interview / 112
  Grooming Considerations / 113
  Clothing for the Interview / 114

Building a Professional Wardrobe on a Budget / 118

7   SUCCESSFUL INTERVIEWING 123

Preparing for the Interview / 124
  Interviewing Questions / 127

Successful Interviewing Tactics / 130
  Dealing with Feelings of Nervousness / 132
  The Importance of Nonverbal Behaviors / 133
  Handling the Interview / 135

Interview Follow-Up / 140

8 NEGOTIATION **147**

Purpose of Negotiation / 148

Assessing and Negotiating a Job Offer / 149
  Assessing the Organization / 149
  Understanding the Job / 150
  Negotiable Factors / 151

Do's and Don'ts in Negotiating / 155

Accepting or Declining a Job Offer / 158

9 PROFESSIONAL COURTESIES IN THE JOB SEARCH **163**

The Importance of Etiquette in the Job Search / 164

Job Search Etiquette / 165

Etiquette in Special Situations / 168
  Phone Interview Etiquette / 168
  Cell Phone Interviews / 169
  Mealtime Interviews / 171

10 DEALING WITH REJECTION **177**

Rejection in the Job Search / 178
  Being Declined Is Part of the Job Search / 178
  Self-Reflection Is Critical / 179

Attitudes for Success / 180
  Keeping a Perspective on Rejection / *181*

Getting Feedback / 182

Self-Evaluation / 185

Creating an Action Plan / 187

Conclusion / 193

Index / 195

Find It Fast

INDUSTRY AND JOB RESEARCH **3**

Looking for ways to learn about professional culture and
become accepted into your field?   See page 13

Want some resources for learning about your industry
or field?   See page 17

**ASSESSING AND DEVELOPING SKILLS
FOR THE WORKPLACE** **25**

Want to know some effective actions to take
to achieve goals?   See page 27

Need some help setting up an internship?   See page 37

Want to learn some strategies for succeeding on an
internship?   See page 37

DEVELOPING A PROFESSIONAL PORTFOLIO **43**

Want to know how to create a learning portfolio?   See page 47

Need an assessment portfolio?   See page 47

Want to create a professional portfolio?   See page 48

NETWORKING AND SELF-PROMOTION **61**

Want some suggestions for successful networking?
See page 64

Need to know networking steps?   See page 69

Want to know how to maximize your networking
effectiveness?   See page 71

Want to know how to create an effective
"elevator speech?"   See page 73

Need suggestions for conducting an informational
interview?   See pages 76–77

RESUME AND COVER LETTER DEVELOPMENT 83

Want some tips on preparing to write your resume?   See page 85

Need some tips on writing an effective resume?   See page 94

Want some steps on cyber-safety when posting
an electronic resume?   See page 96

DRESSING FOR SUCCESS 107

Want to make a good first impression?   See page 109

Need some tips on grooming for an interview?   See page 114

Want some dressing tips for men?   See page 115–116

Want some dressing tips for women?   See page 117

Looking for ideas on how to dress on a budget?   See page 119

SUCCESSFUL INTERVIEWING 123

Want some tips on preparing effectively for an interview?
See page 127

Need some suggestions for participating effectively in
an interview?   See page 132

Need some advice on addressing feelings of nervousness
during an interview?   See page 133

Curious about effective nonverbal communication during
an interview?   See pages 134–135

Want to know methods for interviewing successfully?
See pages 138–139

NEGOTIATION **147**

Need to prepare for negotiating a job offer?   See page 154

Want to know how to successfully negotiate a job offer?
See page 157

PROFESSIONAL COURTESIES IN THE JOB SEARCH **163**

Want to know appropriate job search etiquette?   See page 167

Need some tips on telephone interview etiquette?
See page 170

Need some tips on etiquette during mealtime interviews?
See page 172

DEALING WITH REJECTION **177**

Want to acquire a realistic mindset for the job search?
See page 181

Want to develop a healthy perspective on rejection during
the job search?   See page 182

Looking for a way to find opportunity in rejection?
See page 182

Need some steps for self-evaluation to improve in the
job search?   See page 186

Want some steps for creating an action plan for developing
job search skills?   See pages 187–188

Preface

CONGRATULATIONS!

If you are reading this book, chances are that you are close to completing your college education and are preparing to seek employment in your field. Your dedication and perseverance are about to pay off as you embark on your career. Congratulations on reaching a significant milestone!

AS YOU VENTURE OUT

You are likely to find that there are many details involved in the job search process. Preparing your portfolio, revising your resume, writing cover letters and other correspondence, and preparing a professional wardrobe are examples of the tasks you will need to complete in preparation for seeking employment. In addition to these tangible elements, you will need to know and practice appropriate interview etiquette, how to respond effectively to certain questions in the interview, and how to present yourself as confident, well prepared, and competent.

HOW WILL THIS TEXT HELP ME?

100% Job Search Success covers topics that are fundamental to successful job-seeking efforts. The following are main themes from the topics that are included in the text. Use these to get a general idea of the book and to see how each topic supports you in a successful job search.

▶ **KNOWING YOURSELF AND YOUR INDUSTRY:** Knowing your interests and abilities will help you find a good match between your professional goals and an employment situation. Understanding the requirements and standards of your field will allow you to carry out your responsibilities according to criteria for success in your profession.

▶ **ASSESSING AND DEVELOPING YOUR SKILLS:** There are certain skills, such as leadership and understanding your strengths and weaknesses, that contribute to your success in the job search. Developing these skills before you embark on your job search will work to your advantage.

▶ **DEVELOPING A PROFESSIONAL PORTFOLIO:** Showcasing your abilities to prospective employers is an important part of the job search. Appropriately selecting and displaying your most successful work will contribute to obtaining the job of your choice.

▶ **LEARNING TO NETWORK AND ESTABLISH PROFESSIONAL RELATIONSHIPS:** A significant factor in the job search is establishing professional relationships. Learning to network skillfully will help you develop relationships and a place in the professional world.

▶ **CREATING AN EFFECTIVE RESUME:** A resume is effective when it influences a potential employer to invite you for an interview. Learning to create an effective resume and complete other types of job-related correspondence will help you establish positive contact with employers.

▶ **DRESSING FOR SUCCESS:** The impression you make with your attire and grooming significantly impacts other aspects of the relationships you build during the job search. Learning to consider your body type, coloring, and acceptable business dress when selecting a professional wardrobe will add to your professionalism.

▶ **DEVELOPING INTERVIEWING SKILLS:** After your first impression, the interview is where the interviewer learns more about you. Attention to the details of successful interviewing is more likely to make you stand out from other applicants and maximize your chances of getting the job.

▶ **NEGOTIATING:** Any job offer that you receive must be compatible with your goals and needs. The ability to negotiate effectively maximizes your chances of reaching an employment agreement that is mutually acceptable to you and the employer.

▶ **DEMONSTRATING PROFESSIONAL ETIQUETTE:** Demonstrating professional etiquette—showing good manners—is also likely to make you stand out in the interviewer's mind. Paying attention to the etiquette of particular situations, such as mealtime interviews, is especially critical.

▶ **DEALING WITH AND LEARNING FROM REJECTION:** Being rejected for a position during the job search is a natural part of the process. Feelings of disappointment are normal, but you can also use the rejection process to learn about yourself and your interviewing skills and to improve your job search skills.

HOW TO USE THIS BOOK

100% Job Search Success is written to actively involve you in developing positive and productive job-seeking skills. The following features will help guide you through the material and provide opportunities for you to practice what you've learned:

▶ **THE "BIG PICTURE:"** The "Big Picture" is provided at the beginning of each chapter. The "Big Picture" is intended to give you an overview of chapter contents related to the other chapters in the text. As you read through the material, you are encouraged to recognize and consider the relationships among the various concepts and information.

▶ **LEARNING OBJECTIVES:** Learning objectives are provided as a guide to the information in each chapter. Use them to identify the important points of each chapter and to understand what you are supposed to learn. Also, use learning objectives as a tool to measure what you have mastered and what you still need to work on. Remember that the learning objectives are a guide and you are encou aged to expand on your knowledge according to your goals and interests.

▶ **TOPIC SCENARIOS:** At the beginning of each chapter, a topic scenario demonstrates the application of chapter concepts to the real world. Use the questions following each scenario to stimulate your critical thinking and analytical skills. Discuss the questions with classmates. You are encouraged to think of your own application ideas and to raise additional questions.

▶ **REFLECTION QUESTIONS:** Reflection questions ask you to evaluate your personal development. Reflection questions are intended to increase your self-awareness and ability to understand your decisions and actions.

▶ **CRITICAL THINKING QUESTIONS:** Critical thinking questions challenge you to examine ideas and to thoughtfully apply concepts presented in the text. Critical thinking questions encourage the development of thinking skills that are critical to efficient performance in school and in the workplace.

▶ **APPLY IT!** Following sections of the text, you will find activities that help you apply concepts discussed in the section to practical situations. Your instructor may assign these as part of the course requirements. If they are not formally assigned, you are encouraged to complete them for your own development. *100% Job Search Success* includes the following three types of activities, each indicated by its corresponding icon.

• **Individual Activities.** Individual activities are directed at your personal development.

REFLECTION QUESTIONS

• How do you use critical thinking in your daily life? In school?
• How do you use creative thinking in your daily life? In school?

? CRITICAL THINKING QUESTIONS

1-1 How do you define critical thinking?
1-2 What are the processes of critical thinking?
1-3 How do you define creative thinking?
1-4 What are the processes of creative thinking?

- **Group Activities.** Group activities typically include projects that are more successfully completed with the addition of several perspectives or broad research. A team effort adds to the success of these learning projects.
- **Internet Activities.** These activities are intended to help you develop online skills. For example, you may research a topic or participate in an online discussion thread.

You may find it helpful to combine the activity types. For example, an individual project may require Internet research. Some individual activities can be adapted to a group activity, and vice versa. Use the activities as guides and modify them in ways that support your learning.

▶ **SUCCESS STEPS:** Success Steps are included throughout the text and provide concise steps for achieving various goals. Success Steps are offered as a summary of steps. Details of each step are discussed fully in the body of the text. Are you looking for success steps to achieve a specific goal? Use the table of contents by topic to locate the steps you need.

▶ **LEARNING OBJECTIVES AND LEARNING OBJECTIVES REVISITED:** Learning objectives, like those provided on course syllabi, outline what you should be learning from the chapter. The learning objectives should guide you to the main concepts of the chapter. Refer back to the learning objectives frequently and pay attention to how chapter material adds to your knowledge related to each objective.

Learning Objectives Revisited provides an opportunity for you to assess the effectiveness of your learning and to set goals to expand your knowledge in a given area. The Learning Objectives Revisited grid and instructions for its use are found at the end of each chapter. The following example is taken from Chapter 1 of the *100% Job Search Success* textbook.

▶ **ITEMS FOR LEARNING PORTFOLIO:** A portfolio is a collection of the work that you have done. A *learning portfolio* is used to track your progress through school and a *professional portfolio* showcases your professional accomplishments. A *developmental portfolio* typically contains documents that illustrate your development over time. A professional portfolio contains finished projects and work that represents your best efforts and achievements and will be the emphasis of the portfolio you create as part of *100% Job Search Success*. Throughout *100% Job Search Success,* there are suggestions to include completed activities in your portfolio. Arranging your portfolio in a way that illustrates your professional development and showcases your best work will be useful for reviewing your progress and demonstrating your abilities.

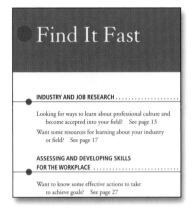

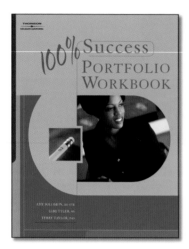

SUPPLEMENTARY MATERIALS

In addition to the textbook, the following accompanying materials are available:

▶ **100% SUCCESS PORTFOLIO WORKBOOK:** This is an optional supplement to the textbook that provides a format for creating your portfolio and expands on the applications of the concepts presented in the text. Elements of the portfolio guide include additional explanations of textbook content, guidelines for keeping a journal, additional professional development resources, and references to online activities.

▶ **THE ONLINE COMPANION:** Textbook and portfolio activities are supported by additional resources located in the Online Companion (OLC). OLC resources include additional activities, assessments, and suggestions for expanding your predevelopment beyond what is included in the textbook. Access the Online Companion at http://www.cengage.com/success/100JobSuccess.

▶ **WEBTUTOR:** The WebTutor is an online course guide that complements 100% Student Success. WebTutor provides you with tools to organize course content, track your progress in the course, and plan your projects. In addition to these organizational tools, the WebTutor provides links to helpful resources, access to discussion threads, and support documents, such as a study sheets, and review quizzes.

BEYOND JOB SEARCH SUCCESS

After you obtain a job, then what? Your first goal is likely to become comfortable in your new position. As you become involved with your organization and profession, you are likely to develop new professional interests and goals. Eventually, you may want to advance in your company and in your field. The next text in the *100% Success* series, *100% Career Success,* provides a foundation for professional development and moving ahead in your field.

The professional skills such as self-management and communication that you learned and developed in school (and practiced as part of *100% Student Success,* if you used that text) are also skills that are desirable to employers. They are also skills that can be applied to finding the job of your choice. *100% Job Search Success* expands on the skills that you have developed by addressing issues specific to the job search process.

A FINAL WORD

Look ahead. As you read and complete the activities of *100% Job Search Success,* keep your long-term career goals in mind. Keep professionalism and etiquette "top of mind" as you go about your job-seeking activities. Application is the key—and the more you practice, the more successful you will be in your job search and in your new position.

Again, congratulations on coming this far in your college career. May you have 100% success on your job search and in the future.

Acknowledgments

The authors of the *100% Success* series would like to thank the staff at Wadsworth Learning for their tireless support and editorial suggestions. Much appreciation also goes out to our students over the years, who have taught us so much. Without them, this book would not have been possible.

We wish to recognize the many educators and students who reviewed various components of the *100% Success* series throughout its development and contributed many thoughtful suggestions for the program.

Dr. Angela Alexander
Nicholls State University
Thibodaux, Louisiana

Douglas Allen
Catawba Valley Community
    College
Hickory, North Carolina

Kim R. Barnett-Johnson
Ivy Tech Community
    College
Fort Wayne, Indiana

Ashley King Brown
Catawba Valley Community
    College
Hickory, North Carolina

Katheleene L. Bryan
Daytona Beach Community
    College
Daytona Beach, Florida

Bettye A. Easley
Grant College, Suffolk
    Community College
Brentwood, New York

Marianne Fitzpatrick
Oregon Coast Community
    College
Newport, Oregon

W. T. Hatcher
Aiken Technical College
Aiken, South Carolina

Irene Gordon Jasmine
Nicholls State University
Thibodaux, Louisiana

Aleyenne S. Johnson-Jonas, M.A.
Brown Mackie College
San Diego, California

Debra M. Klein
Suffolk County Community
   College
Selden, New York

Sara L. Morgan
Minnesota School of
   Business–Plymouth Campus
Minneapolis, Minnesota

Kevin Pugh, M.S.Ed.
University of Colorado
   at Boulder
Boulder, Colorado

Susan R. Royce, M.S.
Design Institute of San Diego
San Diego, California

Leo Sevigny
Lyndon State College
Lyndonville, Vermont

Avette D. Ware
Suffolk County Community
   College
Selden, New York

CHAPTER OUTLINE

Understanding Your Industry and Place within It

Professional Socialization

Sources for Industry Research

Staying Current and Updated

1

Industry and Job Research

LEARNING OBJECTIVES

By the end of this chapter, you will achieve the following objectives:

▶ Describe the personal characteristics and industry elements needed to secure a niche in an industry or field.

▶ Describe the elements of professional culture.

▶ Describe the process of professional socialization and employ steps in the professional socialization process.

▶ Use suggested resources and techniques for researching industries and organizations.

▶ Use suggested resources and techniques for staying updated and current in an industry.

TOPIC SCENARIO

Barbara Schenley is completing her final semester of her college program. She is beginning to consider employment possibilities. Barbara has maintained high grades and has been a successful student. As she prepares to leave the familiar surroundings of her school, Barbara has some concerns about finding her place in the professional world. She is concerned about finding a position that is right for her in an appropriate environment. She is apprehensive about fitting in with her field's professional culture.

Based on Barbara's situation, answer the following questions:

▶ What personal elements should Barbara consider in finding the "right" position?

▶ With which professional requirements does Barbara need to be familiar?

▶ What elements of professional culture does Barbara need to consider in her desire to fit in?

▶ What steps can Barbara take to develop her awareness of her field's professional culture?

▶ What resources can Barbara use to research her industry and specific organizations within it?

▶ Once Barbara is established in her field, how can she remain updated and informed?

UNDERSTANDING YOUR INDUSTRY AND YOUR PLACE WITHIN IT

Understanding your industry and its expectations will facilitate your transition to the workplace and support you in defining your professional role. Finding your place within your chosen profession will be a process that takes into account your interests, professional goals, and abilities. It will also include an understanding, acceptance, and assimilation of professional requirements and values. Knowing the expectations of entry-level positions in your field is important and will contribute to your success as well as prevent disappointment.

YOUR INTERESTS

As you become exposed to more aspects of your profession, you are likely to find certain elements more interesting than others. For example, a nursing student may find that she has a preference for pediatric nursing as opposed

1

to critical care nursing. That student's interest would contribute significantly to establishing her place within the nursing profession. Keep a record of your interests and resources for pursuing them. Interests can—and should—change over time. You can expect to develop and refine your interests over the course of your career.

apply it

Interest Journal

GOAL: **To identify your professional interests and establish resources that support their continued development.**

STEP 1: Create a hard copy or electronic journal. Select a format that is easily accessible to you, suited to your preferences, and one that you will use consistently.

STEP 2: Record your observations regarding the development of your professional interests as they become clear to you. Note significant influences and events that affect your interests.

STEP 3: Include activities, such as interest inventories and other assessments, that contribute to your insights about your interests. Your student services or career placement personnel can be sources of these types of inventories. Record the contact information for mentors and professional colleagues who may be influential in helping you pursue your interests and goals.

STEP 4: Remember that the development of professional interests is a process that will continue during your academic preparation as well as throughout your career. Use this journal as a basis for your future professional growth and development.

YOUR ABILITIES

Specialized areas of a single profession provide a variety of opportunities for individuals with different skills and abilities. For example, an individual who has strong mathematical skills may choose to pursue a more quantitative path in her field than a person with strong verbal skills would. It is important to make an honest assessment of your skills and abilities and select the branch of your field where they will best be utilized.

YOUR VALUES

You are more likely to be happy in your work if the requirements of your position match your values. For example, if being with your family is a high priority, a position that requires travel five days a week may not be your best choice. Determine those values on which you can compromise, those that you can't, and seek a position that is the best fit.

YOUR PERSONALITY

Personality traits such as assertiveness, patience, and risk-taking orientation and preferences for a certain type of work environment will influence the position you seek in your field. For example, if you are an extroverted individual who enjoys contact with and learning from other people, you will be most suited to (and probably happiest in) a position that offers those elements and related opportunities. Comfort zones can be stretched to a certain extent, but being in a situation that challenges your basic personality traits can interfere with your effectiveness on the job.

INDUSTRY REQUIREMENTS

Although you might have specific interests and excellent skills in a certain area, many fields have specific requirements for working in that area or performing certain tasks. These can range from specific experiences to certifications and continuing education units (CEUs). Some of these requirements, such as experience and certification, are summarized here. There may be others, depending on your field.

Experience

Some fields require specific experience as part of the requirements for a job. For example, some allied health fields require a specific amount of direct patient care experience before an individual can teach allied health students at the postsecondary level. Knowing the experience requirements of your industry that may affect your job research and pursuits will support you in seeking the experience you need to realize your long-term goals. Some entry-level positions may require experiences such as internships, part-time work, or involvement in a cooperative education setting.

Certifications

A wide variety of certifications are available in many fields. Some, such as nursing licenses, are required. Others, such as certain technical certifications, may serve as an additional credential that enhances your marketability. Some organizations may require or prefer specific certifications. In some fields, having a minor course of study that complements your major can be an asset. Familiarize yourself with the required and preferred certifications in your field. Your program chair or advisor should have this information available for you. Be prepared to pursue additional certifications if requested by a potential employer or if it is a standard in your industry. Certifications can lead to increased salary, greater opportunity for advancement, and recognition in your field. In some cases, certifications may be required to meet safety and other standards.

Continuing Education

In a world where information and technology change on a constant basis, it is critical that your skills remain up to date. Continuing education, or courses taken after graduation while in the workplace, is one method by which professionals stay apprised of changes in their field and informed of current practices. Continuing education opportunities are available through professional organizations, local colleges, and professional publications. Continuing education requirements are frequently linked with maintaining current certification, which in turn may be required in order to practice in your field. Continuing education requirements vary according to the profession. Familiarize yourself with the specific requirements in your field.

apply it

Professional Requirements Research

GOAL: To increase awareness of professional development resources and processes.

STEP 1: Identify the professional organization(s) that defines certification and continuing education requirements for your field. Instructors and your program chair can assist you in finding this information.

STEP 2: Locate the organization's Web site. Explore the site to find the requirements for certifications and continuing education. Include entry-level requirements such as minimum degree requirements and others such as internships. Make a note of the requirements.

STEP 3: In addition to the requirements, note resources such as publications, e-mail lists, and other tools that you can use to remain informed of continuing education and other professional development opportunities.

1

▶ REFLECTION QUESTIONS

- What other elements might be included in industry requirements?
- What other transferable skills can you identify?
- How effective are your transferable skills? Which ones would you like to develop or improve?

? CRITICAL THINKING QUESTIONS

1–1. How can you determine the quality of your transferable skills?

1–2. How can you develop your transferable skills? Where would you find resources?

1–3. How can you acquire transferable skills while in college?

Transferable Skills

Transferable skills are those skills that pertain to all fields and are appropriately used in all settings and most situations. Examples of transferable skills include effective written and oral communication, the capability to manage people, and self-management skills. Transferable skills may also be referred to as interpersonal skills, "soft" skills (the ability to get along with people), or generic abilities.

PROFESSIONAL CULTURE

Webster's Online Dictionary (2005) provides several definitions for *culture*. While a general definition of culture includes elements such as belief systems, artistic works, and traditions, culture can pertain specifically to the professional setting. The culture of a company is the tone or feeling that is predominant in the organization. It is a product of expectations, standards, the quality of interpersonal relationships, and general atmosphere. Culture ultimately influences the effectiveness and efficiency of the organization. As an example, think about an organization or workplace you were in that felt positive and productive. Compare and contrast this image with a company or organization where the atmosphere was negative and perhaps even demoralizing. A corporate culture that nurtures a positive environment is typically productive and profitable. The following elements contribute to the culture of a profession or organization.

Dress Standards

Every profession has its own standards for appropriate dress. Within each field, dress standards may vary according to position. Dress contributes to culture by defining the impression an employee's appearance conveys. In some fields, casual dress contributes to an easy-going and informal environment. In others, more business-like attire, such as suits, creates a more formal atmosphere. Of course, dress is not the only element that constitutes culture, but it is a significant component. Remember that how you dress will determine in part how you are accepted into your professional or organizational culture. Learn and follow your organization's dress requirements. When attending a professional meeting or conference of professionals in your field, research dress expectations prior to attending.

Interpersonal Relationships

Deal and Kennedy (1982, p. 98) describe the *cultural network* as an informal, yet powerful, communication system that exists within an organization. The relationships and unofficial, casual communication within a profession or organization can significantly influence morale and attitude. It is important to be aware of the influence of informal communication and to use the cultural network in a constructive manner. For example, the informal network can be used to promote supportive and collaborative relationships or, conversely, to pass gossip that can be disruptive and harmful. Your thoughtfulness and judgment in participating in the cultural network can have a significant impact on how you are viewed by your colleagues and accepted into your professional and organizational culture.

Relationships in the workplace are affected by the way you communicate with others. Gain respect from and establish trust with your colleagues by avoiding gossip, rumors, and other questionable interactions. Communication that is honest yet tactful and based on verifiable information is most likely to contribute to effective and productive workplace relationships. Be approachable and open while maintaining a professional demeanor.

Your manner of communicating and participating in the informal corporate culture can have a significant impact on how you are viewed by your colleagues.

Communication Practices

For our purposes, *communication practices* will refer to more formal expression within a profession or organization. The chain of command, processes for making requests and suggestions, and protocols for conflict resolution are examples of formal communication practices. Organizations and professions typically have published policies and procedures for these types of communications. Examples include the policy governing e-mail use in the workplace and a standard format for submitting a weekly report. Your awareness of these practices and your ability to use them effectively will also influence your success in finding your niche within the field or in an organization and fitting in with its culture. Following communication protocol is important to establishing effective working relationships.

Professional Authority

Each profession recognizes knowledgeable individuals and credible sources of expert information and advice in the field. Examples of professional authorities might be your professional organization, individuals recognized as experts in your field, or your supervisor. Likewise, organizations also have their lines of authority, which are referred to as the chain of command. Knowing your sources of professional information and expertise and using them appropriately to validate your activities and contributions will add to your credibility as you find your place within your field. Develop the ability to disagree respectfully and to substantiate your perspective with reliable data. For example, if you believe a deadline for a project is unrealistic, address the issue with your supervisor (or appropriate individual) and

1

substantiate your request for additional time with evidence of other assignments that you are in the process of completing.

Professional Values and Ethics

Values are those elements that an individual or organization holds as important. Examples of values include altruism, loyalty, peace, integrity, and wisdom (Ethics Resource Center, n.d.). Values are the basis of an individual's or organization's vision. When they are shared by group members, they provide a powerful foundation for prioritizing activities, making decisions, and formulating action (Industrial College of the Armed Forces, 1999).

Ethics are the embodiment of certain values and define ways in which individuals carry out values as reflected in daily activities. It is likely that your field will have its own set of values and a professional code of ethics that is based on universal principles and that is intended to guide your professional decisions and actions. Ethics are the translation of principles that guide behavior. They are not absolute rules, but serve as guidelines that provide a basis upon which actions can be determined and conflicts resolved according to the greatest good of the group or individual (Josephson Institute of Ethics, n.d.).

? CRITICAL THINKING QUESTIONS

1–4. What ethical issues can you identify in current events?

1–5. How does the consideration of ethics influence the decisions made about these events and their outcomes?

apply it

Values and Ethics in Practice

GOAL: To translate professional values, ethics, and standards into action.

STEP 1: Form a group of students interested in exploring professional values and ethics and how they are incorporated into daily practice in your field.

STEP 2: Ask each group member to obtain a copy of your profession's code of ethics, standards of practice, values statements, or other documentation of these aspects of your profession. These can be found online, or you may ask a faculty member or librarian for assistance in locating a copy. Consider using general business ethics if you have significant difficulty locating a field-specific code of ethics.

STEP 3: Ask group members to write their thoughts on how the values, ethics, and standards of your field are demonstrated in daily professional activities. One way to think about this is to ask yourself what actions demonstrate these values and how these actions can be incorporated into the tasks of your field.

STEP 4: Meet as a group and share your ideas. Combine them into a group statement of guidelines for actions and behaviors that reflect professional values and ethics.

STEP 5: To obtain feedback, share your final project with a faculty member or other professional from your field.

Professional values may differ from the personal values that you hold individually. Professional values reflect universal, socially responsible principles such as respect, responsibility, and integrity and are the concepts upon which ethics are based. Personal values are those values that reflect your individual belief system. Professional decisions and choices should be made based on universal values (Josephson Institute of Ethics, n.d.). Conflict between personal and professional values must be resolved by referring to your profession's values and its code of ethics. Decisions should be based on these values and on the code, with the interest of your clients in mind. Understanding your profession's code of ethics and being able to apply it to your daily practice is one method of establishing your professional integrity.

PROFESSIONAL SOCIALIZATION

Professional socialization is "a process by which individuals learn the knowledge, skills, values, roles, and attitudes associated with their professional responsibilities" (Pitney, 2002, Introduction, para. 1). Teschendorf (2001) discusses how professional socialization is a gradual process that involves effort. While professional socialization has traditionally been emphasized in the health care professions, the concepts of professional socialization can apply to all employees who are developing their professional identity and establishing their place within their field.

Your professional socialization process will be unique and will involve your becoming acquainted with both formal and informal aspects of your field and the organization for which you work. Consider the following guidelines to facilitate your professional socialization process, adapted from the works of Teschendorf (2001), Pitney (2002), and Deal and Kennedy (1982):

▶ **Establish reliable information sources.** Reliable information about your profession or organization can come from your professional organization, from a trusted individual, or from a combination of dependable sources. From these sources, pay attention to the expected behaviors and attitudes of your field and/or organization and how these are demonstrated in daily activities.

▶ REFLECTION QUESTION

- What values would you identify as most important to an organization? Why did you choose these values?

? CRITICAL THINKING QUESTIONS

1–6. How can a set of professional values be instilled in a large group such as an organization or profession?

1–7. How can you ensure that your decisions and actions are ethical?

1–8. What happens when your personal values come into conflict with your profession or the values of the organization that hired you?

1–9. How will you resolve conflicts between your personal and professional values?

Both informal and formal communication and mentoring will contribute to your professional socialization.

1

▶ **Pay attention to role models.** Another technique for becoming socialized into your professional role is to observe individuals who are experienced and successful in the profession or organization. There is much to be gained by informal learning, such as observing accepted practices and incorporating them (with judgment) into your own behaviors. Ensure that role models meet the criterion of being a reliable source.

▶ **Understand the history and current status of your profession and organization.** Learning the history and current status of your profession or organization can provide insight into its rituals, values, authority distribution, work relationships, politics, and communication practices. Understanding these processes and finding your role within them will support your transition into a new environment.

▶ **Know professional standards.** Your profession is likely to have standards for how tasks are to be accomplished and ideas that have been established and accepted. Professional socialization includes adopting these standards into daily practice. Standards are based on professional values and ethics, so it is important to understand the values underlying your profession as well as its code of ethics. Some professions, such as occupational therapy, incorporate practice expectations into a written document. An example is *Standards of Practice for Occupational Therapy.* Other standards may be less formally stated.

▶ **Look for professional socialization opportunities.** There are numerous opportunities that can provide both formal and informal learning. Some examples that are frequently available to students include information from your academic training, organizational orientations, and other organized learning situations, such as participating in a work environment as part of academic preparation. Chapter 2 will emphasize the internship, which has been identified as an effective method of professional socialization.

▶ **Join professional organizations.** Consider becoming a member of your field's professional organization or the student division of the professional organization. For example, public relations students can join the Public Relations Society of America (PRSA) or the Public Relations Student Society of America (PRSSA) if their school does not have a chapter. Professional organizations frequently offer material and information specifically for students, can be a source of scholarships, and offer an opportunity to become involved with activities in your field. Many organizations offer reduced membership rates for students.

success steps

FACILITATING THE PROFESSIONAL SOCIALIZATION PROCESS

1. Establish reliable information sources.
2. Pay attention to role models.
3. Understand the history and current status of your profession and organization.
4. Know professional standards.
5. Look for professional socialization opportunities.

SOURCES FOR INDUSTRY RESEARCH

There are a variety of resources available to you for researching your industry or profession. Many of these resources can also be used for researching individual companies. Resources are available on your campus, in your local community, and on the Internet, from national and international sources. Information that will be helpful to you in researching a specific company includes a contact person, company history, recognition the company has received, and current projects and goals. Knowing the company's values and mission is also important. Consider the following suggestions for researching your field and specific companies.

THE INTERNET

The Internet provides a vast array of resources for researching various industries and companies. Hiring statistics, salary ranges, and other information can be accessed on the Web. If you know the URL of a specific site that can provide the information you need, access the site directly. If you don't have a specific URL, conducting a search using key terms can provide a significant amount of information. The following are suggested search terms for researching various aspects of your industry:

- industry research
- Bureau of Labor and Statistics
- salary surveys
- hiring statistics
- your profession (for example, "physical therapy" or "computer programming")

If you are seeking information about a specific geographic location, conduct a search using the name of the city or town of interest. Look for the Chamber of Commerce Web site or the official Web site of the city or town. These Web sites often have employment information for the area. Be aware of other sites that might offer useful information.

Individual companies can be researched in similar fashion using the Internet. Conduct a search using "researching individual companies" as your search term. Look for companies such as Hoover's (http://www.hoovers.com) that provide information about organizations in a variety of industries.

Internet research can provide you with important information about your field and organizations in which you have an interest.

GOVERNMENT SOURCES

The federal and state governments often have information related to hiring trends, projections for demand in various fields, and salary information. The Bureau of Labor Statistics (http://www.bls.gov) is the federal department that provides this type of information.

PROFESSIONAL ORGANIZATIONS

A professional organization is composed of individuals within a certain profession or trade. Professional organizations are typically formed at the international, national, and state levels. These organizations will usually have information specific to your field, including technical updates, changes in certification requirements, and legislative updates on issues relevant to

1

the profession. If you are not currently familiar with your field's professional organization, faculty in your department may be able to provide you with the organization's name and contact information. Since professional organizations are more focused on your field than are general Web sites and government sources, the organization can usually provide more specific and accurate information about your field and the specialty areas within it. For example, an automotive trade journal will be able to speak in depth about various specialties and techniques related to engine repair and maintenance. The information can be expected to be accurate and reliable.

NETWORKING

Networking refers to making contacts with individuals from whom you can learn about your profession in general or about specific opportunities within your field or locale. Although you may meet networking contacts in informal situations, effective networking requires more than an informal approach. Careful planning and organization can add to the effectiveness of your networking efforts. Networking is discussed in detail in Chapter 4. Bguides.com (2005) makes the following suggestions for successful networking:

▌ Have a networking plan.

▌ Be aware of networking opportunities as they present themselves (often in unexpected places).

▌ Put yourself in situations where you will meet people.

▌ Communicate effectively.

▌ Develop quality relationships.

▌ Stay organized and express gratitude to individuals who assist you.

▌ Enjoy yourself and have fun with the networking process.

Networking is often an effective method of researching employers, as many positions are not advertised. For example, employment needs are often communicated by word of mouth in professional circles. Being visible increases your access to these types of situations. Also, networking is often a more comfortable environment, as the formality and pressure of a formal interview are absent.

Relationships built through the networking process can provide you with information to develop your professional knowledge and contacts.

INFORMATIONAL INTERVIEWS

Informational interviews are formal appointments in which you interview a professional to obtain specific information regarding your field or the organization as part of your research efforts. As with networking, you will need to be prepared and organized by obtaining appropriate background information, having specific goals for the interview, and formulating

1

relevant questions. You will need to set a specific appointment time, limit your interview to 20 or 30 minutes, and diligently adhere to that time frame. It is appropriate etiquette to send a handwritten thank-you note following the interview. To learn more about conducting informational interviews, use an Internet search tool with "informational interviews" as your search term. Informational interviews are covered in greater depth in Chapter 4.

FACULTY

As instructors, your faculty members are well informed of current news and techniques in your field. They are familiar with local and national professional organizations as well as local facilities and businesses that hire in your field. Consider exploring options with your faculty members. Inform them in advance of the information you are seeking and set an appointment time so that both of you are prepared for the meeting.

CAREER SERVICES

Most schools have a department devoted to assisting new graduates in exploring and locating employment opportunities. Career placement personnel are knowledgeable about current hiring trends, practices, and opportunities, both locally and in other areas, and are also familiar with specific organizations. In addition to resume writing, interviewing skills, and career interest assessments, career services personnel may be able to assist you with organizational research. Consider setting an appointment with a career services representative at your school. Don't wait until you are a graduating senior to take advantage of the benefits of career services. Visit career placement personnel during your first semester so you can apply their advice while you are in school.

PROFESSIONAL JOB COUNSELORS

There are numerous off-campus services that offer professional job and career counseling. Many do in-depth assessments of your interests, aptitudes, and personality factors that can influence your career planning. They may also provide coaching in writing resumes, setting up informational and hiring interviews, and completing other aspects of industry and job research. Keep in mind that these services can be costly. Professional job counselors can be found in your city's telephone directory or on the Internet. If you choose to use a specific counselor or service, be sure to research its history of service and to obtain references.

LIBRARIES

Reference librarians in your school or at the public library are familiar with numerous resources. Consult with reference librarians for assistance in researching areas of interest within your field.

apply it

Sources for Industry Research

GOAL: To establish a method and resources for conducting industry research.

STEP 1: Select a method for recording and collecting resources you find during this activity. Be creative in selecting a method or combination of methods that is easily accessible and that you will use. For example, you may wish to establish an electronic folder in which you bookmark important Web sites, but you may devise a paper filing system for the business cards of professional contacts.

STEP 2: Record and/or file contact information for professional organizations, government sites, professional contacts, and other sources. Remember to select an organizational system that works for the materials you are organizing.

STEP 3: Keep your files updated as you receive new information and add new contacts.

STAYING CURRENT AND UPDATED

In today's information age, all professions grow and change at a rapid pace. In order to remain up to date in your field, it is essential that you have access to current information regarding technical skills, ethical and legal issues, and other elements that contribute to professional culture.

The same resources that provided information on industry and organizational research can also be used for obtaining updated information, provided the source is current. In addition to these resources, there are others that you can employ that will automatically provide you with current information. Consider the following resources for remaining current in your field.

PROFESSIONAL ORGANIZATIONS

Professional organizations exist for the benefit of their professional members. Commitments that professional organizations make to their membership include providing continuing education opportunities, communicating technical developments in the field, and serving other general interests of constituents. Membership in your field's professional organization will typically provide you with access to new information and revisions to existing information, allowing you to remain current in your field. For example, members of a professional organization are typically informed of technical advances and political issues affecting their field. Professional organizations focus on collecting information and disseminating it to their members.

PROFESSIONAL PUBLICATIONS

Professional organizations usually publish an official journal or newsletter that informs readers of developments and research relevant to the field. In addition to publications from your professional organization, there are numerous journals and other materials from related fields that can provide a broader perspective on your industry. As you progress in your professional development, you may become aware of related publications that will support your interests and goals. For example, teachers may find journals on child development a helpful supplement to professional teaching publications.

CONTINUING EDUCATION AND CONFERENCES

One of the benefits of being a member of a professional organization is that you will also receive information about workshops, seminars, and other continuing education opportunities. Some fields require a specific amount of documented continuing education. In other cases, professionals pursue formal learning events to expand their knowledge and interests or to explore new areas. Professional conferences, frequently sponsored by professional organizations, can be excellent sources of learning, as numerous choices of events in one place offer a variety of learning opportunities for one registration fee. Professional conferences can also provide excellent networking opportunities.

CERTIFICATION AND LICENSURE BOARDS

Fields that require a license or certification to practice will typically have a credentialing organization that administers certification activities. Licensure requirements vary from state to state and are monitored by the individual states. Certification organizations and state licensure boards typically communicate updates of policies, requirements, and regulations to individuals holding credentials. Organizations and state boards also have Web sites and contact information; contact them with any questions or concerns regarding professional credentials.

Keep a record of information from professional journals and seminars to develop your knowledge of your field.

1

Some fields require a criminal background check prior to becoming certified. The certification board in your field can provide information regarding whether criminal background checks are a routine practice. It is important to be aware that what you do now can affect your opportunities in your field. For example, drug use or other forms of illegal behavior on your record can prevent you from obtaining the position of your choice.

ELECTRONIC COMMUNICATION

Electronic communication enables nearly immediate and efficient communication via e-mail, electronic mailing lists, and Web forums. Many professional organizations use e-mail to communicate with members. For example, an organization might send weekly e-mails summarizing events of the week. Web-based forums allow members to post questions and to share ideas related to their field. Electronic mailing lists such as LISTSERV or Yahoo! Groups allow information to be posted to a designated group. These services typically require a subscription and may be free or available for a fee. Check with your professional organization for electronic communication tools that the organization might offer.

! RESOURCE BOX

RESOURCES FOR REMAINING CURRENT IN YOUR FIELD
- professional organizations
- professional publications
- continuing education and conferences
- certification and licensure boards
- electronic communication

apply it

Program Resources

GOAL: To establish a community resource for industry research.

STEP 1: Assemble a group of students from your program. Participants should be interested in developing a community resource that will support other students in researching your field.

STEP 2: Research and collect industry resources as described in the previous activity, "Sources for Industry Research."

STEP 3: Assemble the resources into a format that can be easily accessed by students. Suggestions include a bulletin board or a notebook within your department. Your school librarian or learning resource center staff may also have suggestions for your particular school.

CHAPTER SUMMARY

As you begin your career, you will find many opportunities for professional growth and development. This chapter focused on how you can use an understanding of your interests, abilities, and the requirements of your field

1

to establish your professional niche. The elements of professional culture were explored as a way of understanding and becoming involved with the processes particular to your field. You also received suggestions for tools, such as professional organization and continuing education options, to research your field and further your professional development.

POINTS TO KEEP IN MIND

In this chapter, several main points were discussed in detail:

- Finding your place within your chosen profession will be a process that takes into account your interests, professional goals, abilities, and an understanding and assimilation of professional requirements and values.

- Several personal and field-specific elements will influence how you determine your place in your field. These include your interests, abilities, experience, transferable skills, and certification and continuing education requirements.

- Finding your place in your field includes understanding your profession's culture. Elements of professional culture include dress standards, the way interpersonal relationships are conducted, communication practices, sources of professional authority, and professional values and ethics.

- Professional socialization is the process by which you will adopt the values and attitudes of your profession.

- Resources for researching your industry and specific companies include the Internet, government sources, professional organizations, networking activities, informational interviews, faculty members, career services, and professional job counselors.

- Resources for remaining current in your field include professional organizations, professional publications, continuing education and conferences, certification and licensure boards, and electronic communication tools.

LEARNING OBJECTIVES REVISITED

Review the learning objectives for this chapter and rate your level of achievement for each objective using the rating scale provided. For each objective on which you do not rate yourself as a 3, outline a plan of action that you will take to fully achieve the objective. Include a time frame for this plan.

1 = did not successfully achieve objective

2 = understand what is needed, but need more study or practice

3 = achieved learning objective thoroughly

	1	2	3
Describe the personal characteristics and industry elements to consider in securing a niche in an industry or field.	☐	☐	☐
Describe the elements of professional culture.	☐	☐	☐
Describe the process of professional socialization and employ steps in the professional socialization process.	☐	☐	☐
Use suggested resources and techniques for researching industry and organizations.	☐	☐	☐
Use suggested resources and techniques for staying updated and current regarding an industry.	☐	☐	☐

Steps to Achieve Unmet Objectives

Steps   Due Date

1. _____   _____

2. _____   _____

3. _____   _____

4. _____   _____

SUGGESTED ITEMS FOR LEARNING PORTFOLIO

Refer to the "Developing Portfolios" section at the front of this textbook for more information on learning portfolios.

▶ Reflection and Critical Thinking Questions: Include your written responses to these questions. Use them to review your development over time.

▶ Interest Journal: This activity will assist you in identifying your professional interests and resources for their pursuit. Keep this information to guide you in your career search and for future professional development.

1

▶ Professional Requirements Research: Develop a bank of professional development resources. Keep this information to guide you in your career search and for future professional development.

▶ Values and Ethics in Practice: The purpose of this activity is to assist you in applying concepts such as professional values, ethics, and standards to daily activities.

▶ Sources for Industry Research: This activity will support you in developing methods and resources for researching your industry in preparation for the job search.

▶ Program Resources: Work with peers to create a professional resource that benefits all of you. In your portfolio, note the process and resources that you use to complete this activity. Conducting a project such as this can be included on your resume as a transferable skill.

REFERENCES

Bguides.com. (2005). The 9 essentials of networking with people and creating more opportunity (2nd ed.). Bguides: Guides to get business done™. Richmond, VA: MaxPitch Media, Inc. Retrieved March 30, 2005, from http://www.bguides.com

Deal, T. E., & Kennedy, A. A. (1982). *Corporate cultures: The Rites and Rituals of Corporate Life.* Menlo Park, CA: Addison-Wesley.

Ethics Resource Center. (n.d.). Definitions of values. Retrieved March 29, 2005. from http://www.ethics.org/values_defined.html

Industrial College of the Armed Forces (Ed.). (1999, Feb.). Values and ethics [Electronic version]. In *Strategic Leadership and Decision Making* (part 4, chap. 15). National Defense University, Institute for National Strategic Studies. Retrieved March 29, 2005, from http://www.ndu .edu/inss/books/Books%20-%201999/Strategic%20Leadership %20and%20Decision-making%20-%20Feb%2099/pt4ch15.html

Josephson Institute of Ethics. (n.d.). Making sense of ethics. Retrieved March 29, 2005, from http://www.josephsoninstitute.org/MED/ MED-1makingsense.htm

Pitney, W. A. (2002, July–Sept.). The professional socialization of certified athletic trainers in high school settings: A grounded theory investigation [Electronic version]. *The Journal of Athletic Training, 37*(3), 286–292. Retrieved March 28, 2005, from http://www.pubmedcentral.nih .gov/articlerender.fcgi?artid=164358

1

Teschendorf, B. (2001). Faculty roles in professional socialization [Electronic version]. *Journal of Physical Therapy Education,* Spring, 2001. Retrieved March 28, 2005, from http://www.findarticles.com/p/articles/mi_qa3969/is_200104/ai_n8935867/print

Webster's Online Dictionary. (2005). Definition: Culture. Retrieved October 26, 2005, from http://www.websters-online-dictionary.org/definition/culture

CHAPTER OUTLINE

Setting Goals for Your Professional Pursuit

Know Yourself

Gaining Experience: The Overview

The Internship

2

Assessing and Developing Skills for the Workplace

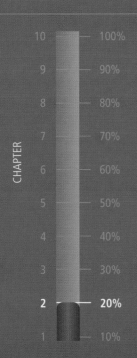

THE BIG PICTURE

LEARNING OBJECTIVES

By the end of this chapter, you will achieve the following objectives:

▶ Define *technical skills* and *transferable skills*.

▶ Define *internship*.

▶ Explain the importance that goals can have on success.

▶ Discuss goals that can be established while in school.

▶ Describe the different types of self-assessment tools.

▶ Discuss the various types of career-building activities that students can utilize to gain experience in their profession.

▶ Explain the purpose and goals of an internship.

▶ Discuss various methods one can use to locate an internship.

▶ Discuss tips on being successful in an internship.

▶ Demonstrate the ability to research possible internship sites.

TOPIC SCENARIO

In her last year of college, Alanna Phillips began to develop her resume. During the process, Alanna analyzed her strengths and identified areas to develop. She discovered the following:

▶ Her college degree had given her a good start on developing the skills necessary for an entry-level job in her field.

▶ Development of some technical skills was still needed.

▶ Soft skills such as communication were effective but still could use some work.

▶ She had learned skills such as negotiating, delegating, and marketing but had no experience in utilizing these skills that could be documented on the resume.

After reaching these conclusions, Alanna decided that gaining further experience using her skills was critical to obtaining the job she wanted after graduation. Alanna began to explore options for obtaining an internship. Based on this short description of Alanna's situation, answer the following questions:

▶ How can Alanna be sure that she has correctly identified her strengths and weaknesses?

▶ How can Alanna be sure that the skills learned in college are transferable to the workplace?

▶ What might Alanna do to identify more clearly what employers in her field are looking for when hiring entry-level employees?

▶ Would an internship help Alanna build on her skills? If so, how might she find out which internship would best benefit her needs and goals?

▶ What type of internship do you think would best serve Alanna's needs?

▶ How can an internship be helpful in promoting oneself to a prospective employer?

SETTING GOALS FOR YOUR PROFESSIONAL PURSUIT

It is important to begin planning and preparing for your professional career while still in school. Being successful and competitive in your profession requires having well-defined goals. In addition to developing your skills and graduating, there are other goals that are important for students to achieve while attending college. These goals should be developed with an appreciation of the influence that both academic and co-curricular experiences can have on overall professional success. Actions that can contribute to goal achievement include the following (Bruce, 2005):

▶ **Make a good impression while in school.** Faculty members, advisors, and other students may be the individuals who recommend you for a job.

▶ **Take leadership roles in and outside of school.** Develop and demonstrate your abilities to work with a variety of individuals. For example, being involved in school activities, community activities, or volunteer work demonstrates leadership and the ability to work with diverse individuals. If you are working in addition to attending school, taking leadership roles on the job also demonstrates this skill.

▶ **Find a mentor who can help guide and promote you and your professional pursuits.** A mentor is an individual who will guide and challenge you to develop both professional and personal skills. This individual may be a faculty member, graduate, or industry professional.

▶ **Be clear on your career objectives.** Develop an awareness of your professional direction and goals. Chapter 1 explored methods for establishing your niche in your profession. Develop career objectives based on where you want to be in your career.

▶ **Understand your strengths and weaknesses.** Explore how your strengths can contribute to your professional growth. Set goals for improving weaker areas. Use feedback from instructors, mentors, academic advisors, and employers to gain insight into your abilities and to set professional goals.

▶ **Gain professional experience while in school.** Participate in volunteer opportunities, co-op work, or an internship to gain experience in your field. Establish and demonstrate a strong work ethic during these opportunities.

---

success steps

ACTIONS FOR GOAL ACHIEVEMENT

1. Make a good impression while in school.
2. Take leadership roles in and outside of school.

continued

▶ **REFLECTION QUESTION**

- What goals do you need to establish that would help in your academic and professional success?

? CRITICAL THINKING QUESTION

2–1. What is your reaction to the following statement? "Goals are important, but because goals change so much, writing them down is unnecessary." Provide a rationale for your response.

continued

3. Find a mentor who can help guide and promote you and your professional pursuits.

4. Be clear on your career objectives.

5. Understand your strengths and weaknesses.

6. Gain professional experience while in school.

KNOW YOURSELF

Identifying and being aware of your existing knowledge, skills, experiences, and character traits is a necessary step toward being able to market yourself successfully. In school, students have the opportunity to use instructors' feedback to develop an understanding of their strengths and weaknesses in both technical and transferable skill areas.

Technical skills are generally thought of as those skills that are necessary to perform specific job tasks. The University of Manitoba Career and Employment Services office (n.d., p. 2) identifies the following *transferable skills,* which are those abilities that can be easily transferred to a variety of work settings. Interpersonal and communication skills are examples of transferable skills.

- analytical/problem-solving skills
- flexibility/versatility
- interpersonal skills
- oral and written communication skills
- organization/planning skills
- motivation
- leadership skills
- self-starter/initiative
- ability to work as part of a team

For future professional success, it is important to evaluate your strengths and weaknesses both in interpersonal skills ("soft skills") and technical abilities and to improve areas as needed during the college years.

SELF-ASSESSMENT TOOLS

Conducting a self-assessment can be both challenging and rewarding. Various assessment tools help students to match their interests, skills, and personality type with their school and career goals. Depending on the outcome of the

©Digital Vision

Knowing your unique and individual traits will help you to market yourself effectively.

various self-assessment tests, individuals may at times find the need to re-evaluate professional goals. Becoming more self-aware may prompt some students to consider other professions that better fit with their strengths, abilities, and personality type. If this is a consideration, students should seek out further guidance from individuals trained in career counseling.

A variety of self-assessment tools are available, often found online. The student services or academic advising department on your campus may also be able to provide resources for these tools. Assessment tools can include the following (University of California at Berkeley Career Center, n.d.):

▶ **Interest inventories.** Interest inventories include the Strong Interest Inventory, the Self-Directed Search (SDS), the Campbell Interest and Skill Survey (CISS), and the Career Key (Dikel, 2002). The Strong Interest Inventory assesses your interests and matches them to careers. The inventory tells you where you might enjoy working, based on the interests you have in common with other individuals in a given profession. The Strong Interest Inventory does not measure ability or aptitude.

▶ **Personality tests.** Myers-Briggs Type Indicator® (MBTI), Keirsey Temperament Sorter, and TypeFocus are examples of available personality assessment tests. These tests can provide information on how you communicate, gather information, and make decisions. They can also help you determine if your personality fits the job that you are considering (Dikel, 2002). TypeFocus helps answers questions such as, "What are my personal strengths?", "What careers will I find satisfying?", and "How do I use my strengths in a successful job search?"

▶ **Skills inventories.** The Skills and Attributes Inventory (SAI) and the SkillScan assessment can help in defining your skills and abilities. SkillScan helps you identify your skills and how they apply to various careers. In addition, it provides the opportunity to identify careers in which your skills are most applicable. The tool also assists you in strategizing to develop your career and in writing your resume to support your goals.

apply it

Self-Assessment Activity

GOAL: To develop a clearer appreciation for and understanding of your strengths and weaknesses.

STEP 1: From the various self-assessment tools mentioned in this chapter, select one.

continued

! RESOURCE BOX

SELF-ASSESSMENT TOOLS
- interest inventories
- personality tests
- skills inventories

▶ REFLECTION QUESTION

- What self-assessment tool interests you the most and why?

? CRITICAL THINKING QUESTION

2–2. What is your reaction to the following statement? "Other than the fact that self-assessment tests are fun to take, there is no validity to them and they are a waste of time." Provide a rationale for your response.

2

continued

STEP 2: Conduct further research regarding this tool and take the test.

STEP 3: Write a brief report regarding your findings and what you discovered about yourself.

STEP 4: Consider placing your self-assessment test in your Learning Portfolio.

GAINING EXPERIENCE: THE OVERVIEW

▶ REFLECTION QUESTIONS

- What career-building activity most interests you?
- What steps do you need to take to begin your search for a career-building activity?

❓ CRITICAL THINKING QUESTION

2–3. How can you determine the activities that are best suited to building your career?

Gaining employment after graduation is a typical goal of many college students. Seeking opportunities in and out of class to develop abilities and skills can significantly increase your employment opportunities. Having experience prior to beginning the job search can significantly increase your credibility and demonstrates commitment to your career choice. Career-building activities can include volunteer work, job shadowing, a part-time job, consulting work, or an internship. Through these activities, students can gain experience in utilizing both their technical and transferable skills.

Gaining experience in your field increases your marketability in the workplace as well as demonstrates your interest in and commitment to your field.

THE INTERNSHIP

In some professions, internships are commonly completed as part of the educational process as an option or, in some cases, as a requirement. Other names for internships include externship, on-site experience, or practicum. All refer to practical experience in the work setting. Loyola Marymount University Career Development Services (n.d., p. 1) defines an internship as "an educational experience whereby students learn to take on meaningful responsibilities within an organization and to adopt roles as contributing employees." Internships can take place at any time during the academic experience or as a capstone experience to classroom learning at the conclusion of academic preparation.

PURPOSE OF AN INTERNSHIP

According to McGill University Career and Placement Service (n.d., "Goals That Internships May Satisfy"), the purposes of an internship may include:

- learning more about a specific industry/field
- gaining practical experience while applying theoretical knowledge
- becoming more knowledgeable about specific work functions and learning career-related skills
- gaining experience working with others and seeing how decisions are made
- developing a relationship with a mentor and cultivating a network of contacts in your field
- increasing your marketability
- performing positive community service
- gaining experience in job-seeking skills, interviewing, and resume and cover letter preparation
- getting to know yourself better

Making the most of an internship is the responsibility of the student. Maximizing learning from the internship experience requires involvement in the process of choosing the best internship possible for personal growth and development. Each student should be directly involved in the internship selection process, regardless of whether the internship is or is not a requirement of the academic program. By being directly involved, the student can effectively meet individual goals. To determine individual internship goals, consider the following elements:

- **Your career interests.** Determine the areas of your field that are most interesting to you. Seek an internship that will provide you

2

the opportunity to explore areas of interest. If you are unsure of your preference, an internship can help you define it by exposing you to various professional situations. Even if the internship is an academic requirement, do not consider it simply as another thing you have to do to graduate. Approach the experience with openness to learning as much as possible.

▶ **The internship environment.** Consider the environment in which you would like to complete your internship. Recall from Chapter 1 factors such as your goals, personality style, values, and the surroundings and atmosphere in which you like to work. Consider the size, philosophy, and other aspects of the potential internship site. Make sure the organization is a match with your internship goals and who you are as a person. Often success in an internship depends on the right fit. Internships can contribute significantly to the process of professional socialization that was discussed in Chapter 1.

▶ **Your current priorities.** Completing an internship requires the same level of commitment expected for a job. It is important to seek an internship experience that allows you to meet other life obligations. Consider the following aspects:

  ▶ **Location.** Whether you stay in your locale or travel across the country for an internship will depend largely on your other commitments. For example, an individual who has family responsibilities may choose to not accept an internship one thousand miles away, even though the internship site supports his interests and is a good fit. Conversely, another individual might make the opposite decision in the interest of gaining the experience. Making these types of decisions is frequently a part of selecting an internship site.

  ▶ **Finances.** Internships can be costly when they are full time (thus limiting available hours for paid employment) and when they have no stipend or other benefits. Benefits vary depending on the internship site. For example, a site might offer the intern a meal at the company cafeteria during her assigned shift. Other sites offer fully paid internships; still others offer a modest stipend. Be aware that paid internships of any kind are becoming less common. Some sites may be able to offer a part-time internship commitment to allow additional paid work hours. It is important to consider your financial priorities as part of internship selection.

  ▶ **Current employment.** If you intend to keep a paid job during your internship, it is important to negotiate a mutually acceptable plan with your employer. Taking a leave of absence or modifying

2

your hours are examples of solutions to balancing your paid work with an internship. Some employers may be able to consider you for a different position in your field upon completion of the internship.

LOCATING THE BEST INTERNSHIP

Once the goals of the internship have been established, the task of locating the best internship to meet those goals begins. If completion of an internship prior to graduation is a goal, then the search should begin as early in the academic process as possible, as an early search maximizes the chances that you will find the best internship to meet your needs. Some students may choose to do a different internship each year during their academic training, depending on the length of the academic program. The following are resources for locating an internship (Hansen, n.d.):

▶ **Career services office.** Nearly all career services offices have a list of their school's internship programs, important application dates, and other sources of internship information. The wide range of resources available in this office makes it an effective place to start your search. Some offices have an internship coordinator dedicated to locating internship sites.

▶ **Major/minor department.** Major-specific internship programs are frequently maintained by the department office. One or more faculty members may specifically handle internships.

▶ **Networking sources.** Tell everyone you know that you are looking for a specific type of internship. Just as with job hunting, networking can be one of your best sources for internships, especially for competitive internships.

▶ **Internship and career fairs.** Most colleges offer at least one career fair during the academic year. Even if you are looking for an internship in a different geographic location, attend the fairs and network with the recruiters. Many organizations have multiple offices, and you may find an opportunity in your area of choice.

▶ **Alumni office.** Many colleges now ask alumni if they would be willing to sponsor current college students as interns. These alums can be a source for internships as well as for networking opportunities.

▶ **Company Web sites.** If you have already identified a specific set of companies where you would like to intern, consider researching them yourself by visiting the career section of each company's Web site.

2

- ▌ **Internship Web sites.** There are a few general internship Web sites, as well as a number of industry-specific Web sites. Conduct a search using the term "internships" or "internship (+ your field)" and explore your results.
- ▌ **Print resources.** Trade magazines, industry journals, and newspapers have advertisements from numerous organizations and companies. Reviewing journals can expose you to new organizations and aspects of your field.
- ▌ **Cold contact.** If other sources have not yielded results, then cold calling is an option. This process can involve calling contacts by phone or sending them an introduction letter to request further information. The phone book may be a source of companies for cold calling.

❗ RESOURCE BOX

EXAMPLES OF RESOURCES FOR ARRANGING INTERNSHIPS
- career services office
- major/minor department
- networking sources
- internship and career fairs
- alumni office
- company Web sites
- internship Web sites
- books and periodicals
- cold contact

▌ REFLECTION QUESTIONS

- What resources do you think you would find the most useful in locating an internship?
- What resource do you not feel comfortable using but believe could be worthwhile? How can you become more comfortable using this resource?
- How do you think you can document your search efforts for an internship? How might this documentation be helpful to you now and in your future job search activities?

apply it

Locating Internship Sites

GOAL: *To demonstrate the ability to locate a variety of internship sites.*

STEP 1: Utilizing the resources suggested in this chapter, conduct research to locate at least three different possible internship sites. (Before doing this, check the protocol in your field. In some professions, internships are arranged strictly between academic staff and site supervisors. If you are in this category, involve your internship coordinator in this activity.)

STEP 2: After locating an internship, call or write to the company to inquire if an internship in is available and what the company's requirements are. Ask for guidance during this process as needed.

STEP 3: Put together a brief report of findings to present to the instructor.

STEP 4: Consider placing the information from locating internship sites in your Learning Portfolio.

Once a number of possible internship sites have been identified, it is important to remain diligent in following through with the necessary calls and letters. Being persistent is important and can make a difference in whether or not you obtain the desired internship. Be sensitive to the employer's time and contact employers only when absolutely necessary during this process.

Preparing well-written resumes, cover letters, and thank-you letters for the internship search is also important.

INTERNSHIP SUCCESS

Success of an internship is up to the employer and the student. If academic credit is to be received for the internship, then the college can also be instrumental in helping to ensure that the internship experience is a success. School personnel can facilitate communication between the site supervisor and the student by initiating requests for necessary documents such as internship time sheets and site supervisor evaluation reports. Ultimately, it is the student's responsibility to follow up and ensure that required tasks and forms are completed and to make his or her internship a beneficial experience.

Certain actions and attitudes on your part will contribute to your learning and success. Maximize the benefits you gain from your internship experience by implementing the following recommendations:

▶ **Be informed.** Knowing what is expected of you by both the school and the internship site is critical to your success. Prior to arriving at the internship site, learn as much as you can about dress codes, schedules, policies, and other relevant aspects of the job. An introductory meeting or telephone call to the internship supervisor or coordinator offers an opportunity for you to introduce yourself as well as ask questions and get relevant information. You are also likely to have an orientation session upon your arrival at the site.

If your internship is part of your academic requirements, there will be standards set by your school or program that you will need to meet. Examples are deadlines for submitting paperwork (which can have a direct influence on your grade or ability to graduate on time) and performance requirements for grades. The internship coordinator on your campus will be able to provide you with relevant information. Be sure to ask questions if anything is unclear.

▶ **Prepare.** Learning as much as possible about the site prior to your arrival will facilitate your transition to the site. For example, learn about the expectations of your role and the types of clients with whom you will work. Learn about the organization and its history. Being prepared will increase your comfort level as you begin your internship as well as demonstrate your initiative and interest.

▶ **Treat the internship as you would a new job.** The internship is where you make your debut into the professional world. Demonstrate the same commitment and investment that you would if you were starting a new job. The internship is similar to a first job and is the ideal place to develop positive professional habits. In addition,

? CRITICAL THINKING QUESTION

2–4. How would you adjust your research tactics if you were trying to locate part-time work, consulting work, or a shadowing experience?

2

It is the student's responsibility to communicate effectively with the internship supervisor and to demonstrate the same professional skills that will be expected on the job.

2

internships are frequently listed on the resume as work experience, and you may be using your internship supervisor as a professional reference. Many interns are hired by the internship site either at the conclusion of the internship or later in their careers.

▶ **Be inquisitive and open to learning.** Demonstrate an interest in your work, the organization's activities, and other events related to the internship site. Be open to learning about new ideas and trying new things. Ask questions. Your interest demonstrates dedication to your work and the organization and a willingness to grow professionally.

▶ **Take responsibility.** The step beyond being inquisitive is to actively seek opportunities for learning. Find organizational and professional activities of interest and become involved rather than waiting to be asked. Be accountable for your actions.

▶ **Use supervision to your benefit.** You will probably have regular meetings with your supervisor to discuss your progress and to discuss any issues that might arise. Use supervision to ask questions, clarify information, and explore areas of interest. Pressing issues should be addressed immediately, but supervision is the appropriate venue for discussion and fostering professional development. Use positive feedback to develop your strengths; accept constructive criticism to set goals for growth and improvement.

▶ **Use your critical thinking skills.** Think through problems and issues objectively and thoroughly. Avoid personal bias and emotional responses that cloud professional judgment. Analyze data and base decisions on rational and verifiable information. Act on ethical principles and in the best interest of clients and the organization.

▶ **Respect professional boundaries and limits in a positive way.** All professionals—including seasoned ones—have limits to their knowledge and expertise. All professionals have room for growth and development. Recognizing what you *don't* know is as important as recognizing your strengths. If there is something you don't know or understand, ask for clarification or assistance, and in doing so, be sure that your attitude reflects your desire to learn. Do not use not knowing or understanding as an excuse for not doing a task. Likewise, professional roles have boundaries. For example, a health aide cannot administer medications, even though she might know how. Medication is administered by a nurse, for regulatory and safety reasons. These types of professional boundaries are in place for liability and management reasons. Understand your professional boundaries, recognize why they exist, and respect them.

REFLECTION QUESTIONS

- What is your response to positive feedback? How can you use it to develop your professional strengths and skills?
- What is your typical response to constructive criticism? How can you use it to set goals and improve areas needing development?

? CRITICAL THINKING QUESTION

2–5. How would you respond if you were asked to do something that was clearly outside of your professional boundaries?

▶ **Pay attention to professional behaviors and standards.** Chapter 1 emphasized the importance of professional ethics and standards. It is your responsibility to know and apply these guidelines to your internship responsibilities. Maintain your awareness of these standards and consciously apply them to your decisions and actions. For example, if you are unsure about the "right" way to approach a problem that arises in your work, consider your professional code of ethics in addition to technical solutions. Consider whether your technical solution is acceptable from an ethical perspective.

▶ **Respect and fit into the organization's culture.** Be a team player. Participate in activities that contribute to a positive environment and work relationships. You might choose one or two activities that are suited to your interests and comfort level. It is important to be visible in your organization in a positive way.

▶ REFLECTION QUESTION

- What will you do to ensure success in your internship experience?

success steps

STRATEGIES FOR INTERNSHIP SUCCESS

1. Be informed.
2. Prepare.
3. Treat the internship as you would a new job.
4. Be inquisitive and open to learning.
5. Take responsibility.
6. Use supervision to your benefit.
7. Use your critical thinking skills.
8. Respect professional boundaries and limits in a positive way.
9. Pay attention to professional behaviors and standards.
10. Respect and fit into the organization's culture.

 apply it

Internship Site Visit Report

GOAL: *To gain a better understanding of the requirements of an internship site.*

STEP 1: Groups of four or five students should each be given information for a prearranged internship site visit. The site should be different for each group.

continued

2

continued

STEP 2: When visiting the site, students should document what is learned about the site, how interns function at that site, and the site's requirements for interns. Students should also inquire into what makes a good intern versus a poor intern.

STEP 3: After the visit, group members should compile their information and prepare a brief report to present to the class.

STEP 4: Consider putting this report in your Learning Portfolio.

 ## CHAPTER SUMMARY

This chapter emphasized the importance of recognizing your strengths and areas needing development and setting goals for professional development in preparation for the job search. You were encouraged to begin this process as early as possible by assuming leadership roles on and off campus, researching and becoming involved in your profession, and networking with individuals in your field. Completing an internship was discussed as a significant means to enter your field and gain experience in the workplace. You reviewed important phases of the internship, including selecting, preparing for, and completing the internship, and you were provided with guidelines for the successful completion of each of the three phases.

 ## POINTS TO KEEP IN MIND

In this chapter, several main points were discussed in detail:

- To be successful and competitive within your profession requires having well-defined goals.
- Technical skills are those that are necessary to perform specific job tasks.
- Interpersonal skills are also known as soft skills and are the type of skills that can be easily transferred to another job or work setting.
- Self-assessment inventories can provide individuals with insight into their interests, skills, and personality type.
- Self-assessment tools include the Strong Interest Inventory, MBTI, TypeFocus, and the SAI.

▶ Gaining experience can provide more credibility and demonstrates commitment to one's career choice. This experience can come through obtaining a part-time job, performing volunteer work, engaging in job shadowing, doing consulting work, or completing an internship.

▶ Being directly involved in the internship selection process can help to ensure your goals are met.

▶ There are a variety of resources available to obtain an internship. These sources include Web sites, books, periodicals, and school officials.

▶ It is up to you, the student, to make the internship experience benefit your future professional success.

LEARNING OBJECTIVES REVISITED

Review the learning objectives for this chapter and rate your level of achievement for each objection using the rating scale provided. For each objective on which you do not rate yourself as a 3, outline a plan of action that you will take to fully achieve the objective. Include a time frame for this plan.

1 = did not successfully achieve objective

2 = understand what is needed, but need more study or practice

3 = achieved learning objective thoroughly

	1	2	3
Define *technical skills* and *generic skills*.	☐	☐	☐
Define *internship*.	☐	☐	☐
Explain the importance that goals can have on one's success.	☐	☐	☐
Discuss various goals one should establish while in school.	☐	☐	☐
Describe the different types of self-assessment tools.	☐	☐	☐
Discuss the various types of career-building activities that students can utilize to gain experience in their profession.	☐	☐	☐
Explain the purpose and goals of an internship.	☐	☐	☐
Discuss various methods one can use to locate an internship.	☐	☐	☐
Discuss tips on being successful in an internship.	☐	☐	☐
Demonstrate the ability to research possible internship sites.	☐	☐	☐

2

Steps to Achieve Unmet Objectives

Steps   Due Date

1. _____   _____

2. _____   _____

3. _____   _____

4. _____   _____

SUGGESTED ITEMS FOR LEARNING PORTFOLIO

▶ Reflection Questions: Include your written responses to these questions. Use them to review your development over time.

▶ Self-Assessment Test: Keep a record of what you discovered about yourself.

▶ Locating Internship Sites: Find and research potential internship sites.

▶ Internship Site Visit Report: Prepare a report on internship requirements at a particular site.

REFERENCES

Bruce, C. (2005). Career advice for engineering & other technical majors. The Black Collegian Online. Retrieved March 8, 2005, from http://www.black-collegian.com/career/engineer.shtml

Dikel, M. R. (2002). A guide to choosing tests that are right for you [Electronic version]. Retrieved March 9, 2005, from the Dow Jones Career Journal Web site: http://www.careerjournal.com/jobhunting/usingnet/20030429-dikel2.html

Hansen, R. S. (n.d.). How to find your ideal internship. DeLand, FL: Quintessential Careers. Retrieved March 8, 2005, from http://www.quintcareers.com/finding_ideal_internship.html

Loyola Marymount University, Career Development Services. (n.d.). Internship guide for students. Retrieved March 9, 2005, from http://www.lmu.edu/careers/Internships/internshipguide.pdf

McGill University, Career and Placement Service. (n.d.). Internships: Finding one that's right for you. Retrieved March 9, 2005, from http://www.caps.mcgill.ca/tools/internships/

University of California at Berkeley, Career Center. (n.d.). Evaluate yourself. Retrieved March 8, 2005, from http://career.berkeley.edu/Plan/Evaluate.stm

University of Manitoba, Career and Employment Services. (n.d.). Getting started. Retrieved March 9, 2005, from http://www.umanitoba.ca/student/employment/resources/search/started.php

2

©Digital Vision

CHAPTER OUTLINE

Purposes of Professional Portfolios

Types of Portfolios

Portfolio Formats

Contents of the Portfolio

Selecting Artifacts

Organizing the Portfolio

Evaluating the Portfolio

3 Developing a Professional Portfolio

THE BIG PICTURE

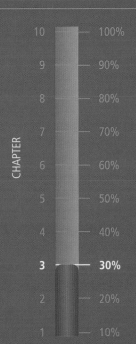

LEARNING OBJECTIVES

By the end of this chapter, you will achieve the following objectives:

▶ Discuss the purpose of developing a professional portfolio.
▶ Describe the different types of portfolios and explain how each fulfills a specific purpose.
▶ Select appropriate artifacts for each of the portfolio types.
▶ Select an organizational strategy appropriate to the type and purpose of the portfolio.
▶ Devise a method of portfolio evaluation.
▶ Assemble the beginnings of a professional portfolio.

TOPIC SCENARIO

Lily Blackstone has numerous projects and documents that she has accumulated over the course of her academic preparation. These items represent her achievements and abilities in a competitive job market. Lily would like to include these examples of her accomplishments in her interviewing process. She is wondering how to do this in a manner that is appropriate and professional.

Based on Lily's situation, answer the following questions:

▶ How can Lily appropriately showcase her projects and achievements as part of the interviewing process?

▶ What criteria should Lily follow when selecting projects and documents to showcase? How should she determine the criteria?

▶ How should Lily present her portfolio to potential employers?

PURPOSES OF PROFESSIONAL PORTFOLIOS

Imagine an artist who is applying for a job as an illustrator. The artist's resume lists an impressive array of previous jobs and describes the artist's skills and abilities. His references from previous employers are all excellent. The potential employer, although impressed with the artist's resume, wants to know that his style fits the illustration criteria of the publisher. The employer looks at the artist's work showcased in his portfolio and makes a decision about the work based on tangible examples.

Internweb.com (2000) points out that although portfolios are familiar in fields such as the creative and visual arts, they are not as well known in other fields. Although less commonly utilized in fields outside of the arts, professional portfolios can benefit job seekers in any profession.

The general purpose of the portfolio is to provide examples of work that an individual can perform. Internweb.com (2000, "Reasons for Using a Professional Portfolio") summarizes the purpose of a professional portfolio as follows: "A strong professional career portfolio provides direct evidence of your related accomplishments. It provides potential employers with a 'snapshot' of your achievements to date, the type of work you've done, and the type of employee you will be. A professional portfolio goes beyond a cover letter and resume. Rather than simply telling an employer about your skills, it provides evidence of them."

In addition to the general purposes listed above, professional portfolios can serve to support other professional goals. Consider the following specific uses for a professional portfolio as defined by Simmons and Lumsden (n.d.):

Your portfolio serves as a vehicle for demonstrating your skills and showcasing your accomplishments to potential employers.

MARKETING YOUR SKILLS IN JOB INTERVIEWS

The professional portfolio can be used as part of the interview process to showcase your abilities and accomplishments to a potential employer. The job history and descriptions and other information included on a resume represent important information that a potential employer definitely needs. The examples of completed work (referred to as *artifacts*) included in the portfolio demonstrate your technical ability, attention to detail, organizational skills, information management abilities, and communication skills.

DOCUMENTING PROFESSIONAL DEVELOPMENT ACTIVITIES

If you are in a field that requires licensure or certification, it is likely that you must submit evidence of continued professional development to keep your credentials current. Institutional and programmatic accrediting bodies typically require evidence of continuing professional development. In addition, there may be other circumstances in which you will be asked for evidence of your lifelong learning efforts. The professional portfolio can provide the documentation of these activities for a variety of regulatory agencies.

GUIDING YOUR PROFESSIONAL DEVELOPMENT

In addition to documenting your continued learning for the purposes of career advancement and regulatory compliance, the professional portfolio provides you with a guide for your personal growth and development. Chapter 1 discussed professional socialization and the process of finding your niche in your field. Creating an effective portfolio can result in your having a tool for recognizing trends in your professional development, setting goals, and developing your professional interests and skills.

SUPPORTING REQUESTS FOR SALARY INCREASES OR PROMOTIONS

The step after becoming established in a position is often to seek a salary increase or to apply for a promotion. In either case, it is important to be able to document your accomplishments to substantiate your request for an increased salary or to demonstrate your ability to assume the additional responsibilities of a promotion. Carefully selected items in the portfolio can demonstrate merit for a raise as well as qualifications for a promotion.

QUALIFYING FOR BONUSES AND OTHER FINANCIAL AWARDS

As with raises and promotions, a portfolio of your achievements can document professional development activities that may be required to be considered for bonuses. Receiving grants for program development and research may also require documentation of your professional activities.

 ## TYPES OF PORTFOLIOS

Several types of portfolios can be used to serve various purposes. Although the various types are usually maintained as separate pieces, elements of each can be used to culminate in a professional portfolio. Three types of portfolios that can be utilized throughout your academic experience and transformed into a professional portfolio for interviewing will be reviewed here.

THE LEARNING OR DEVELOPMENTAL PORTFOLIO

Barrett (2001) and Springfield (n.d.) discuss the learning and developmental portfolios, respectively. Artifacts in these types of portfolios serve the purpose of documenting your development over time. They typically include written reflections on what you have learned and how your learning contributes to your professional development, and they are kept on an ongoing basis to document development. Springfield (n.d.) points out that the personal and "unrefined" nature of the material in this type of portfolio usually renders it inappropriate for use in an interview or other professional situation. It may be possible, however, to translate some of the material from the developmental portfolio into a piece that supports the professional portfolio. Developmental portfolios can be continued throughout your career as a vehicle for reflection and personal growth. Developmental or learning portfolios may also be called "working," "reflective," or "self-assessment" portfolios.

success steps

CREATING AN EFFECTIVE LEARNING OR DEVELOPMENTAL PORTFOLIO

1. Select artifacts that illustrate your development over time.
2. Include reflections on what you have learned and how artifacts contribute to your professional growth.
3. Refine materials into a finished format when you want to include them in a professional portfolio.

THE ASSESSMENT PORTFOLIO

Assessment portfolios are collections of work that demonstrate achievement in a course, program, or project (Barrett, 2001; Springfield, n.d.). Assessment portfolios can be effective measures of "soft" skills such as critical thinking and problem solving; reflective and self-assessment processes may also be a large component of the assessment portfolio. Like the developmental portfolio, some of the material may be too unrefined for inclusion in a professional portfolio; however, the content of these less refined items may contribute to the more polished artifacts to be presented in professional circumstances.

success steps

CREATING AN EFFECTIVE ASSESSMENT PORTFOLIO

1. Focus on one area of professional development.
2. Include artifacts that illustrate your development in this area.
3. Include reflections on how the activities have contributed to your growth in the area of focus.
4. Refine materials into a finished format to be included in a professional portfolio.

THE PROFESSIONAL OR CAREER PORTFOLIO

The professional or career portfolio is the main focus of this chapter. This type of portfolio represents your best work and examples of your highest achievements. These are the polished pieces that will effectively market you to a potential employer or represent your accomplishments in other professional

3

circumstances. Springfield (n.d.) suggests that you use items from the developmental and assessment portfolios as contributing material to your professional presentation. Also, if you use reflection or assessment items, use each one for a specific purpose and relate each to a specific goal or accomplishment.

> ### success steps
>
> **CREATING AN EFFECTIVE PROFESSIONAL PORTFOLIO**
> 1. Include examples of your best work and highest achievements.
> 2. Use portfolio materials to support your resume and the presentation you make to a potential employer.
> 3. Relate reflections to a specific professional goal or achievement.

> **REFLECTION QUESTIONS**
>
> - How could you use a portfolio to enhance your learning immediately?
> - How might you use a portfolio in the future?

Use all three types of portfolios, shown in Table 3–1, to contribute to your professional development, both in school and in your career. Remember that all types of portfolios can be effectively used in all stages of your career. For example, a developmental portfolio can document your ongoing professional growth and learning after graduation. An assessment portfolio can document your achievement in a continuing education course. As you develop professionally, your career or professional portfolio of accomplishments will also change. Use the various types of portfolios during different stages of your career to best achieve your current professional goal.

apply it

Portfolio Research

GOAL: *To increase your familiarity with different portfolios and their uses.*

STEP 1: Conduct an Internet search using the terms "professional portfolios" or "career portfolios." Review the results for articles that will be helpful to you.

STEP 2: Create a file of important tips and ideas that you find in the articles. Consider creating a file of hard copies of the articles or bookmark them in an electronic file. Use your file as a reference when creating your own portfolio.

STEP 3: Consider sharing and exchanging resources with classmates who are also completing this activity.

STEP 4: Add your list of resources to your Learning Portfolio.

TABLE 3–1 TYPES OF PORTFOLIOS

Type of Portfolio	Uses	Important Elements
The Learning or Developmental Portfolio	Document learning and professional development and over time	Artifacts: ▶ document a sequence of learning or professional progress in a specific area ▶ typically include written reflections on what you have learned and how your learning contributes to your professional development
The Assessment Portfolio	Demonstrate achievement in a course, program, or project	Artifacts: ▶ can assess "soft" skills such as critical thinking and problem solving ▶ typically include reflective and self-assessment processes
The Professional or Career Portfolio	Represents best work and examples of highest achievements	Artifacts: ▶ are the polished pieces that will effectively market skills to a potential employer ▶ represent accomplishments relevant to professional circumstances

PORTFOLIO FORMATS

Professional portfolios can be in electronic format, hard copy, or presented in a combination of both formats. Each has its advantages and disadvantages, and the format you select will depend on your field, the type of material you are presenting, and your intended audience. Various formats are presented in the following paragraphs; select the most appropriate based on your situation.

ELECTRONIC FORMATS

Electronic portfolios are those that use a variety of electronic technologies such as videotapes, sound bites, and other visual or audio enhancements, including computer-readable media (Barrett, 2001). Barrett differentiates the electronic portfolio from the digital portfolio, in which all elements are in computer-readable form only, and lists the following advantages of the electronic portfolio:

▶ more easily stored and uses minimal storage space
▶ easily updated and backed up
▶ efficiently transported or transmitted electronically
▶ increases and demonstrates your technical skills
▶ may be more appropriate in highly technical fields

Disadvantages include:

- The recipient must have the equipment to use the electronic item.
- The recipient must have compatible software for digital media.
- The recipient must have the expertise to use electronic formats.
- Electronic portfolios may not be appreciated or effectively reviewed in less technical fields.

HARD COPY PORTFOLIOS

Hard copy portfolios are collections of documents and other media. Many hard copy portfolios are organized in a three-ring binder, which is recommended so that the contents can be easily changed and revised (Shalaway, 1999). The advantages of the hard copy portfolio include:

- easy reading, due to traditional format
- requires no special equipment or expertise
- may be more appropriate in fields where technology is not a typical medium of communication

Disadvantages include:

- bulkiness; more difficult to transport or send
- takes up a greater amount of storage space
- may be seen as outdated in highly technical fields

COMBINATION PORTFOLIOS

You may have some portfolio artifacts that lend themselves to an electronic format and others that are more appropriate in hard copy. Consider the advantages and disadvantages of each, as well as the format that will present the information most effectively. If possible, find out as much as you can about the individual who is reviewing the portfolio and his or her preferences. Finally, consider other elements that are unique and relevant to your situation. Weigh all of these factors in determining the most effective format for your portfolio.

CONTENTS OF THE PORTFOLIO

Professional portfolios typically contain items commonly used to document professional development. Simmons and Lumsden (n.d.) suggest putting the following artifacts in a professional portfolio:

- resume or curriculum vitae

Your choice of a method for storing and presenting your portfolio will depend on the type of material, your audience, and other considerations specific to your field. You may select an electronic format, hard copy, or a combination of both.

- transcripts
- documentation of professional memberships and affiliations
- documentation of professional licensure and other credentials
- letter of reference and recommendations
- documentation of specific skills, such as speeches, acceptance letters for presentations, awards, and other commendations
- samples of work, such as reports, designs, completed projects or their outcomes, and other tangible results of your efforts. Note that certain work samples may be best presented in person; others, electronically. This is an example of when you will need to select the best format for your material.

Contents should be presented neatly, correctly, and professionally. Carefully review portfolio contents for appearance and accuracy. Portfolios should be reviewed with the same level of critical objectivity that one would use in reviewing a resume or other professional document.

SELECTING ARTIFACTS

Selecting the contents of the portfolio should be a thoughtful process focused on achieving your objective. The completed portfolio should clearly illustrate the story you are telling about yourself. It should be organized in a logical order rather than being a haphazard group of documents collected in one place (Shalaway, 1999). The artifacts that you select for your portfolio will depend on the portfolio type, its intended use, and your objectives. In general, ask yourself the following questions when determining which artifacts to include in your portfolio:

- What is my objective in creating this portfolio? What am I documenting?
- Which of my work samples will reflect what I desire to document?

THE PROFESSIONAL OR CAREER PORTFOLIO

When compiling a professional or career portfolio, select artifacts that demonstrate your professional abilities. Ask yourself the following questions of each artifact:

- Is the artifact of excellent quality?
- Is the artifact polished and professional?

? CRITICAL THINKING QUESTION

3–1. Considering your field and situation, which format would best fit your needs? (Consider electronic, hard copy, or a combination.) Explain the rationale for your choice.

©Image Source Limited

Review your portfolio contents carefully to ensure accuracy, thoroughness, and a professional presentation.

▌ Does the artifact reflect and document the development of skills required for the position?

▌ How do reflections and assessment materials contribute to my objective?

▌ Are reflections and assessments presented appropriately and professionally?

THE LEARNING OR DEVELOPMENTAL PORTFOLIO

When compiling a learning or developmental portfolio, artifacts should reflect your progress toward a specific goal. The following questions can help you determine artifacts to include in your developmental portfolio:

▌ Does the artifact demonstrate a significant step in professional growth?

▌ Is the artifact relevant to the skills needed for a specific goal?

▌ Do the reflections that you include relate to the professional developmental process?

▌ Do the reflections demonstrate thoughtfulness and insight about your own growth and goal achievement?

THE ASSESSMENT PORTFOLIO

Assessment portfolios are intended to demonstrate achievement of specific objectives, such as completion of a project or course. Because artifacts included in this type of portfolio are intended to show progress and assess your growth, the artifacts may not be "perfect" initially. Artifacts may include assessments of your progress over time, and your reflections will show evidence of your learning and development. Answering the following questions can help you determine content for an assessment portfolio:

▌ Is the artifact related to achievement of the objective?

▌ Does the artifact show progress toward the objective?

▌ Do assessments demonstrate progress toward the objective?

▌ Do reflections demonstrate an awareness of professional growth toward the objective?

▌ Does the artifact reflect and document the development of skills related to the objective?

apply it

Entry-Level Position Requirements

GOAL: To determine appropriate examples of work to include in a professional portfolio.

STEP 1: Research an entry-level position in your field. Consider a specialty area that interests you. Focus on the skills that employers require and prefer for someone entering that particular specialty.

STEP 2: Review your courses, assignments, and projects. Select those assignments that best reflect the skills that are required.

STEP 3: Decide how you would best represent these projects in a professional portfolio. For example, would you select an electronic or hard copy format? What elements of the finished project would you include to demonstrate your skills?

STEP 4: Consider keeping your developing professional portfolio artifacts in your Learning Portfolio.

Use the following table to determine the contents for the type of portfolio you have chosen.

CHECKLIST FOR PORTFOLIO CONTENTS

Type of Portfolio	Contents Checklist
General Portfolio Considerations	▶ What is my objective in creating this portfolio? What am I documenting? ▶ Which of my work examples will reflect that which I desire to document?
The Professional or Career Portfolio	▶ Is the artifact of excellent quality? ▶ Is the artifact polished and professional? ▶ Does the artifact reflect and document the development of skills required for the position? ▶ If I include reflections or assessment material, how do they contribute to my objective? ▶ Are reflections and assessments presented appropriately and professionally?
The Learning or Developmental Portfolio	▶ Does the artifact demonstrate a significant step in professional growth? ▶ Is the artifact related to the skills related to a specific goal? ▶ Do any reflections that you include relate to the professional developmental process? ▶ Do reflections demonstrate thoughtfulness and insight about your own growth and goal achievement?
The Assessment Portfolio	▶ Is the artifact related to achievement of the objective? ▶ Does the artifact show progress toward the objective? ▶ Do assessments demonstrate progress toward the objective? ▶ Do reflections demonstrate an awareness of professional growth toward the objective? ▶ Do the artifacts reflect and document the development of skills related to the objective?

apply it

Preparing for the Professional Portfolio

GOAL: *To gather potential artifacts for the professional portfolio.*

STEP 1: Using the information in this chapter, prepare a list of potential items specific to your field that you would include in your professional portfolio.

STEP 2: Research credentials and other requirements of your field. Professional organizations and state licensing boards are usually good sources for this information.

STEP 3: Construct a chart or timeline that indicates the criteria for achieving the credential and the time frame for achieving it. Pay special attention to those credentials that are required for entrance into professional practice or those that would enhance your chances of obtaining your position of choice.

STEP 4: Create a checklist of steps you need to take to complete each credential. Include contact information and deadlines related to each step.

STEP 5: Consider including the checklist in your Learning Portfolio and referring to it as a guide for compiling this aspect of your professional portfolio.

ORGANIZING THE PORTFOLIO

Portfolios should be organized in a manner that supports the "story" you are telling. Simmons and Lumsden (n.d.) suggest that most portfolios are organized functionally or chronologically. Your choice of organization will depend on the type of portfolio and its objective.

FUNCTIONAL ORGANIZATION

Functionally organized portfolios are arranged by skill area. For example, if you wish to showcase your management skills, then artifacts demonstrating these skills would be grouped together. Functional organization of a portfolio is similar to the functional resume, which lists achievements according to skill area. Functional organization is appropriate for professional portfolios or for a developmental portfolio that documents your development in a set of areas. Assessment portfolios may be organized by topic to document achievement by function.

CHRONOLOGICAL ORGANIZATION

Portfolios that are organized chronologically are arranged according to the sequence in which the artifacts were completed or milestones were achieved. For example, a portfolio showing progress in a single course might be organized with artifacts from the beginning of the course through the end. Chronological portfolios can be used as one would use a chronological resume (achievements listed in the order they were accomplished) and are commonly used to demonstrate development and growth over time.

EVALUATING THE PORTFOLIO

It is important to evaluate the effectiveness of your portfolio in terms of how it meets its intended objective. Portfolio evaluation should occur before you present it in professional circumstances, in order to ensure that it is complete and appropriately configured. Evaluation methods should also be used periodically to ensure that your portfolio is keeping pace with your professional growth. Evaluate your portfolio by answering the following questions:

▮ How completely were my objectives met? What evidence do I have to show that my objectives were met? *How* were they met?

▮ Does the organization of the portfolio serve its purpose?

▮ Do the artifacts effectively tell my story? Do I need to add any artifacts? Should any be removed?

▮ What responses and comments does an objective reviewer provide about the portfolio's contents?

CHECKLIST FOR PORTFOLIO EVALUATION

▮ How completely were my objectives met?

▮ What evidence to I have to show how they were met?

▮ Does the organization of the portfolio serve its purpose?

▮ Do the artifacts effectively tell the "story" that is intended?

▮ Do any artifacts need to be added?

▮ Do any artifacts need to be removed?

REFLECTION QUESTION

• What other criteria might you use to evaluate the effectiveness of your portfolio?

3

apply it

Portfolio Evaluation Checklists

GOAL: *To prepare a targeted evaluation checklist for professional portfolios.*

STEP 1: Form a small group of students from your class.

STEP 2: Using the general portfolio evaluation checklist on page 53, expand the evaluation to be more detailed and specific to your field. Create your evaluation items based on criteria appropriate to someone entering your field. Consider what an employer would desire and create items that will guide and evaluate the selection of artifacts accordingly.

STEP 3: Consider including the finished evaluation form in your Learning Portfolio.

apply it

Beginnings of a Professional Portfolio

GOAL: *To start a professional portfolio that can be used in the job search process.*

STEP 1: Using the steps outlined in this chapter, devise a plan for creating your professional portfolio. You may also use the results from the other activities in this chapter for this process.

STEP 2: Research and find the resources you will need to create the artifacts that you wish to include. For example, if you want to include a videotape in your portfolio, how will you create the videotape?

STEP 3: Begin assembling the materials and resources that you will need to complete your professional portfolio. Realize that this is a long-term endeavor. It is helpful to view this activity as a process over time.

STEP 4: Consider keeping the developing artifacts, or a record of developing the artifacts, in your Learning Portfolio.

CHAPTER SUMMARY

This chapter introduced you to professional portfolios as a tool for showcasing your professional skills and achievements. You learned various types of portfolios, appropriate contents for each, and how to use each type of portfolio effectively. The goal and purpose of the portfolio was a major theme throughout the chapter, and you received guidelines for selecting artifacts based on the purpose of the portfolio. Portfolio formats and organization were also emphasized, and you received guidelines for selecting an appropriate format and effectively arranging portfolio contents.

3

POINTS TO KEEP IN MIND

In this chapter, numerous main points were discussed in detail:

- ❱ The general purpose of the portfolio is to provide examples of the work an individual is capable of.
- ❱ Portfolios can serve different purposes. The types of portfolios include the professional or career portfolio, the developmental or learning portfolio, and the assessment portfolio.
- ❱ Professional portfolios can serve to support other professional goals, such as obtaining salary increases and promotions, achieving professional credentials, and qualifying for professional development milestones and awards.
- ❱ Professional portfolios can be in electronic format, hard copy, or a combination of both.
- ❱ Professional portfolios typically contain items commonly used to document professional development, such as a resume, transcripts, documentation of recognition, and examples of work.
- ❱ Selecting the contents of the portfolio should be a thoughtful process directed toward achieving your objective. The completed portfolio should clearly illustrate the story you are telling about yourself.
- ❱ Portfolios are typically organized functionally or chronologically. Portfolios should be organized in a manner that supports the story you are telling.
- ❱ It is important to evaluate the effectiveness of your portfolio in terms of how it meets its intended objective. Evaluation can occur prior to using the portfolio to ensure its completeness and after its use to determine its effectiveness.

3

LEARNING OBJECTIVES REVISITED

Review the learning objectives for this chapter and rate your level of achievement for each objective using the rating scale provided. For each objective on which you do not rate yourself as a 3, outline a plan of action that you will take to fully achieve the objective. Include a time frame for this plan.

1 = did not successfully achieve objective

2 = understand what is needed, but need more study or practice

3 = achieved learning objective thoroughly

	1	2	3
Discuss the purpose of developing a professional portfolio.	☐	☐	☐
Describe the different types of portfolios and explain how each fulfills a specific purpose.	☐	☐	☐
Select appropriate artifacts for each of the portfolio types.	☐	☐	☐
Select an organizational strategy appropriate to the type and purpose of the portfolio.	☐	☐	☐
Devise a method of portfolio evaluation.	☐	☐	☐
Assemble the beginnings of a professional portfolio.	☐	☐	☐

Steps to Achieve Unmet Objectives

Steps   Due Date

1. _____   _____

2. _____   _____

3. _____   _____

4. _____   _____

SUGGESTED ITEMS FOR LEARNING PORTFOLIO

▶ Portfolio Research: This activity will help you to select the right portfolio for your needs by increasing your familiarity with different portfolios and their uses.

▶ Preparing for the Professional Portfolio: The goal of this activity is to gather potential artifacts for the professional portfolio.

▶ Entry-Level Position Requirements: This activity will help you determine appropriate examples of work to include in a professional portfolio.

▶ Portfolio Evaluation Checklists: These activities will help you to prepare a targeted evaluation checklist for professional portfolios.

▶ Beginnings of a Professional Portfolio: The goal of this activity is to help you start a professional portfolio that can be used in the job search process.

REFERENCES

Barrett, H. C. (2001). Electronic portfolios [Electronic version]. *Educational Technology: An Encyclopedia.* ABC-CLIO. Retrieved April 13, 2005, from http://electronicportfolios.com/portfolios/encyclopediaentry.htm

Internweb.com (2000). Portfolios: A secret weapon for your internship search. Retrieved April 12, 2005, from http://www.internweb.com/portfolios.asp

Shalaway, L. (1999). The professional portfolio. Excerpted from L. Beech (Ed.), *Learning to Teach . . . Not Just for Beginners.* New York: Scholastic, Inc. Retrieved April 13, 2005, from http://teacher.scholastic.com/professional/futureteachers/professional_port.htm

Simmons, A., & Lumsden, J. (n.d.). Portfolio preparation guide. Florida State University, Career Center. Retrieved April 12, 2005, from http://www.career.fsu.edu/ccis/guides/port.html

Springfield, E. (n.d.). Student portfolio uses. University of Michigan School of Nursing. Retrieved April 13, 2005, from http://www-personal.umich.edu/~espring/ePort/stuPfolios.html

CHAPTER OUTLINE

What Is Networking?

Networking Venues

Steps in the Networking Process

Other Networking Techniques

4 Networking and Self-Promotion

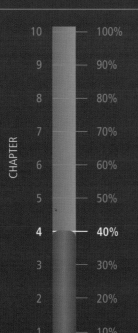

THE BIG PICTURE

CHAPTER

10	100%
9	90%
8	80%
7	70%
6	60%
5	50%
4	**40%**
3	30%
2	20%
1	10%

LEARNING OBJECTIVES

By the end of this chapter, you will achieve the following objectives:

▶ Define *networking* and describe what it is not.
▶ Describe the purposes of networking.
▶ Describe various networking venues and how each is best utilized.
▶ Practice steps of effective networking in various settings.
▶ Implement strategies to increase the effectiveness of networking.
▶ Implement additional networking techniques such as informational interviewing.

TOPIC SCENARIO

Roger McPherson has been job hunting for several months, but with few results. His frustration reached an all-time high when he heard from a career counselor that many advertised jobs are filled long before they are advertised in print or on the Internet. The career counselor told him that he needed to network and make connections in the field as a way to promote himself effectively.

Based on Roger's situation, answer the following questions:

▶ What did the career counselor mean by "networking" and "making connections"?

▶ What did the career counselor mean when he told Roger to "promote himself effectively"?

▶ Where are some places that Roger might begin his networking?

▶ What are some important points for Roger to remember as he begins networking?

▶ How should Roger organize his networking efforts?

WHAT IS NETWORKING?

There are many definitions and descriptions of networking. "Networking is about meeting people . . . and finding that person or persons who has an interest in your skills, background, and what you can bring to a company" (Kovar, n.d.(a)). Bguides.com (2005) states that "networking is simply building relationships . . . with the understanding that each of you represents a valuable resource with expertise to share." Essentially, networking is establishing relationships and contacts, sustained over time, that benefit both parties in the professional world. In the case of seeking job referrals and a niche in the professional workplace, networking is typically directed at establishing relationships that can lead to employment opportunities and professional growth.

Briefly, networking involves meeting people who can provide you with pertinent information and referrals and to whom you can provide the same or something comparable. Obtaining information and getting referrals may involve face-to-face meetings, telephone conversations, or e-mail correspondence (Kovar, n.d. (b)). The remainder of this chapter will focus on how to engage in successful networking.

WHAT NETWORKING IS *NOT*

Effectively describing networking may begin with an explanation of what it is not. Several sources describe common misconceptions of networking. Networking is not:

▶ Calling the people you know when you need a job (Flantzer, n.d.). You may get lucky using this approach, but results are not likely to be as effective or long term as they can be with true networking.

▶ Telling people how wonderful you are (Bjorseth, as cited in Kovar, n.d.(b)). While a part of networking does involve promoting yourself and your skills, self-promotion is directed at demonstrating how your skills can meet the needs and support goal achievement of others.

▶ Getting a referral from everyone you talk to Kovar (n.d.(b))). You can expect a certain number of rejections and/or individuals who are unable or unwilling to assist you in your networking efforts. Effective networking takes time, patience, and persistence.

▶ All about you (Kovar, n.d.(a); Flantzer, n.d.; Welch, n.d.; Kurow, 2002). Although you are likely to benefit from networking, it also involves giving support to others. Networking relationships are mutually beneficial. You must add value to your networking relationships by giving in return to people you meet during the networking process.

Professional networking results in mutually beneficial relationships in which you give and receive information that supports professional development.

4

WHAT NETWORKING IS

Networking is the establishment and maintenance of mutually supportive professional relationships over time. Establishing a network to belong to that provides mutually beneficial results takes time, commitment, and attention. Networking means having relationships with a variety of people who can provide information and resources to each other. Consider the following aspects of successful networking, recommended by Kovar (n.d.(b)) and others:

▶ **Successful networking depends on long-term relationships.** Bguides.com (2005) emphasizes that in order to successfully network, you must think beyond specific events and one-time contacts. Networking entails building relationships that are sustained and involve mutual exchange between people over time.

▶ **Networking occurs over a sustained time period.** It is unlikely that you will achieve a lead for employment (or other information) during a single contact or at one particular time. Patience and persistence are necessary for successful networking. Establishing the effective relationships upon which successful networking is built requires time as well as maintaining contact with the individual.

▶ **Successful networking requires courtesy and respect.** Courtesy and consideration are of paramount importance in professional networking. You demonstrate consideration in part by being respectful of busy schedules, offering something of value in return, demonstrating effective listening skills, and expressing appreciation.

▶ **Research and knowledge are critical elements of networking.** It is important to research the industry or organization in which you have interest or with which your contact is involved. Kovar (n.d.(b)) suggests the Internet as a tool for conducting effective research. Refer to Chapter 1 for an in-depth discussion on conducting company- and field-specific research.

---

tips and tricks

GUIDELINES FOR SUCCESSFUL NETWORKING

- Successful networking depends on long-term relationships.
- Networking occurs over a sustained time period.
- Success in networking requires courtesy and respect.
- Research and knowledge are critical elements of networking.

THE PURPOSE OF NETWORKING

Networking can serve a variety of purposes. Although as a college student your main focus for networking is likely to be finding employment, keep in mind that the concepts of networking can be applied to a variety of situations and may serve you well at various times throughout your career. The following purposes of networking are adapted from Flantzer (n.d.):

▶ **Networking provides knowledge.** If you have a working knowledge of your field and its trends, you are more likely to be prepared to present yourself effectively to potential employers. Also, if corporate downsizing affects you at some time in your career, current knowledge of trends in your field will prepare you to be more aware of your options.

▶ **Networking provides contacts for employment.** Networking puts you in contact with individuals who may be able to hire you or refer you to a potential employer. Use your knowledge of your field to present yourself as informed and skilled. Networking provides the opportunity for you to communicate how your skills can benefit a potential employer's organization.

▶ **Networking establishes mutually beneficial relationships.** The networking process also introduces you to individuals who might benefit from your connections and knowledge and with whom you can establish mutually beneficial relationships. By positioning yourself in a way that allows you to help others, you set the stage for exchanging information that can benefit you and your contacts. Professional organizations are excellent resources for obtaining current industry knowledge, as well as for making professional contacts.

NETWORKING VENUES

Networking venues are typically of two types: those that exist and those that you create (American Association of Retired Persons, n.d.). Existing venues include established businesses and organizations where your skills might be needed. Networks that you create might include contacts that you make at networking or social events and that represent a wide variety of organizations.

EXISTING NETWORKS

Using an existing network means going to an event sponsored by a specific organization or conducting an informational interview with an individual at

4

the organization. Utilizing an existing network offers a more focused approach to networking but may not present the diversity that created networks can provide. Existing networks are most useful when you are pursuing a position in a specific organization or seeking a niche in a particular field. The following are examples of existing networks:

- an existing business or organization
- an industry-specific career fair
- your field's professional organization

©Image 100 Ltd.

Networks can be created and developed from a variety of social and business settings.

CREATED NETWORKS

Created networks are those that you develop from a wide variety of sources. For example, you may attend a social event, attend a conference, and go to dinner with friends in another industry. You establish a relationship with an individual from each of these venues. You follow up appropriately and take the steps to maintain effective networking relationships (these steps will be discussed later in this chapter). By taking these steps, you have created a network. Created networks may take longer and more energy to establish than existing networks but can be richer in what they can offer because of their diversity. They are most useful for someone who wishes to explore different fields, is looking for a change, or would like to apply his or her skills in a new area. Created networks can be formed from any activity or venue where you are interacting with other people. Some of the more formal venues include:

- non-industry-specific career fairs
- professional organizations outside of your field
- networking groups and mixers
- Chamber of Commerce events

STEPS IN THE NETWORKING PROCESS

Incorporating the elements of successful networking can be accomplished by following basic steps and organizing your endeavors around those steps. Chapter 1 briefly summarized the steps of the networking process as it relates specifically to the job search process. The same steps will be reviewed here and then be described in greater depth and applied in a more general manner. Consider how you can ensure that each of the elements of successful networking can be integrated into your networking plan.

Chapter 1 included suggestions for successful networking from Bguides.com (2005). Here, those suggestions are discussed in detail.

- **Have a networking plan.** Know what you are seeking and have a goal in mind. Clarify the information you need and steps you need to take to achieve your objective. Know the types of people who can provide you with valuable information, and seek to meet those individuals. Determine the types of settings and events where you can best achieve this. From this information, devise a plan for your networking.

- **Be aware of and prepared for networking opportunities as they present themselves (often in unexpected places).** It is important to be prepared for networking opportunities as they present themselves. You are more likely to recognize opportunities when you have prepared an effective networking plan. Based on your plan, be prepared with a personal introduction, questions that will engage the individual and encourage conversation, open-ended questions that will lead to the information you are seeking, and a closing statement that expresses appreciation for the person's time and information. You may or may not request an opportunity for follow-up.

▶ **REFLECTION QUESTION**

- What other networking venues can you think of? List as many as you can.

? **CRITICAL THINKING QUESTION**

4–1. How can you learn about upcoming and organized networking events in your area?

4

4

Networking can occur in any situation, including those where you might not expect it. For example, social events and informal gatherings can present excellent networking opportunities.

▶ **Put yourself in situations where you will meet people.** Effective networking requires interaction with others. Involve yourself in activities where you are likely to meet new people. Activities can be professional or social.

▶ **Communicate effectively.** Effective communication requires effective nonverbal and verbal messages. Be aware of how others perceive your facial expressions, eye contact, general energy level (which should not be too low and yet not overwhelming), and gestures. Rely on your plan and the questions you have prepared to sound polished and professional. (Avoid sounding like a recording.) Use effective listening skills and ask pertinent, open-ended questions. Remember that both nonverbal and verbal communication can have different meanings to individuals from diverse cultures. Be sensitive to cultural preferences and perceptions.

▶ **Develop quality relationships.** The key to effective networking is the quality of relationships rather than the quantity of relationships. Keep your goals in mind so that you can foster relationships that support them. Quality relationships are based on developing a mutual understanding of individual needs and goals and providing information that supports them. Remember to add value to your relationships by giving back.

▶ **Stay organized and support individuals who assist you.** Be organized. After you meet someone, make notes regarding his or her affiliation, expertise, and interests, along with other pertinent information about your meeting. In addition to supporting your goals, you will have information about the person and may be able to offer something related to his or her interests and goals.

▶ **Follow up appropriately.** It is essential to follow up any networking activity with a handwritten thank-you note. Thank your contacts for referrals, information, and other assistance that they provide. It is also courteous to express appreciation for someone's time and effort, even if no specific referrals or leads came from the information. If you are in doubt regarding whether to send a thank-you note, it is best to err on the side of sending one. Expressing appreciation is always acceptable.

▶ **Enjoy yourself and have fun with the networking process.** Meeting people is fun and can support your current interests as well as spark new ones. You may discover new aspects of yourself or your profession. Approach networking with an open mind and spirit of adventure.

success steps

NETWORKING STEPS

1. Have a networking plan.
2. Be aware of and prepared for networking opportunities as they present themselves (often in unexpected places).
3. Put yourself in situations where you will meet people.
4. Communicate effectively.
5. Develop quality relationships.
6. Stay organized and support individuals who assist you.
7. Follow up appropriately.
8. Enjoy yourself and have fun with the networking process.

apply it

A Networking Plan

GOAL: To establish a plan for successful networking.

STEP 1: On a sheet of paper or in an electronic document, list the elements of preparing to network. These steps, adapted from Bguides.com (2005), include the following:

   a. your goal

   b. steps you need to take to achieve your objective

   c. information you need,

   d. types of people you need to meet

   e. types of settings and events where you might meet these people

STEP 2: From your list, and based on the resources available in your locale, determine specific networking venues, identify people who fit the types you have defined, and research information that you will need to be well prepared.

STEP 3: In preparation for actually networking, record contact information for individuals and registration information for events.

MAXIMIZING YOUR NETWORKING SUCCESS

Sustaining relationships over time requires investment of time and energy. In today's busy world, it is unreasonable to expect that someone you have met briefly will remember you. However, if you have stayed in touch and given back it may be more likely that people will think of you when they encounter someone who might be helpful to you. Consider the following suggestions for maintaining your visibility with the contacts that you make:

▶ **Make others feel valued.** Welch (n.d.) tells us that "people may not remember what you say or do. They will always remember how you make them feel." Pay attention to contacts' accomplishments and attributes that merit recognition. Give sincere compliments and respect for achievement and successes.

▶ **Demonstrate thoughtfulness.** Considerate actions can make an impression. Gestures that are done in another's best interest and without expectation for reward are typically appreciated and remembered. Zucker (n.d.) gives the example of sending someone information about a conference in his or her field with a brief note stating that you thought the person might be interested in learning about it. Another thoughtful gesture is to send an article or Internet link to someone on a topic of interest. If you have done and organized your networking notes on the contacts you have made, this should be a fairly easy task.

▎ **Stay connected.** Zucker (n.d.) emphasizes the importance of staying in touch with people on a continual basis. Sending holiday cards with an update on your activities is one way to accomplish this. Another way to keep in touch with contacts is to send an e-mail or other correspondence regarding changes you have made or other information about your professional life that your contacts might find interesting. People are flattered that you included them in your correspondence, and doing so keeps your name in front of them.

▎ **Focus on what you can offer others.** Let your contacts know what you can bring to their organization. Kurow (2002) reminds us that people are typically most interested in how you can help them. Maintain a clear picture of the contributions you can make based on your skills and talents and be able to express how these meet your contacts' needs. Use what you have learned in your research to understand your contacts' needs and be prepared to demonstrate how you can help them.

▎ **Get involved.** Being involved in a variety of organizations outside of your profession can benefit you by increasing your visibility, exposing you to a variety of new people, and showcasing your abilities (Zucker, n.d.). Consider taking prominent roles in community and other organizations of your choice.

4

success steps

MAXIMIZING YOUR NETWORKING SUCCESS

1. Make others feel valued.
2. Demonstrate thoughtfulness.
3. Stay connected.
4. Focus on what you can offer others.
5. Get involved.

❓ CRITICAL THINKING QUESTION

4–2. How can you begin to implement networking steps and activities to create a strong network for your job search?

apply it

Networking Preparation

GOAL: To prepare for effective networking.

STEP 1: Prepare a list of topics related to your field on which you would like information. Also, prepare a brief introduction of yourself and your goal.

STEP 2: Prepare a list of open-ended questions related to your topics that would be appropriately asked of a networking contact. If you need help with questions, conduct an Internet search using "professional networking" as your search term and look for articles that suggest effective open-ended questions.

STEP 3: Familiarize yourself with the questions you decide on so that you are comfortable and effective using them when the appropriate situation arises.

STEP 4: Practice with classmates, friends, or other individuals who will give you honest and constructive feedback.

apply it

Simulated Networking

GOAL: To practice presenting yourself effectively during a networking opportunity.

STEP 1: Set aside a time with classmates to hold a "networking event." You may set this up as part of a class activity or as an event held after school hours either on or off campus. You may find it effective to involve other students by requesting the assistance of your career services department.

STEP 2: Make appropriate arrangements according to the plans you have made.

STEP 3: Attend the event as you would any other networking event. Practice the steps outlined in this chapter and use them during the event.

STEP 4: Although this is a *simulated* activity, be aware of opportunities that can present themselves. Remember that opportunities can be found anywhere.

OTHER NETWORKING TECHNIQUES

There are other techniques that can add to your networking skills. Networking opportunities can present themselves at any time, and you will need to be prepared. Other situations may require a more formal approach. Methods that you can use in both of these circumstances are presented here.

THE ELEVATOR SPEECH

An elevator speech is a "short (15–30 second, 150-word) sound bite that succinctly and memorably introduces you" (Kurow, 2002). The name *elevator speech* is derived from the idea that you should be able to deliver your introduction and make a lasting impression in the time it takes to ride an elevator. Elevator speeches are also sometimes called "30-second commercials." You should highlight your unique qualities and their benefits in your elevator speech, and do so in an assured and conversational manner.

You can use your elevator speech anytime and anywhere you wish to introduce yourself to a potential contact and spark his or her interest. Typically, you can use your elevator speech when anyone asks you the question, "What do you do?" Elevator speeches can be used in a variety of settings from formal networking events to standing in line at the grocery store. Kurow (2002) makes the following suggestions for devising an elevator speech:

▶ **Consider the benefits that you can deliver.** You are more likely to evoke interest if your elevator speech clearly identifies the benefits of what you do. The advantages you can deliver are likely to capture the attention of your contact and lead to further conversation. List all your services and their benefits.

▶ **Create a captivating opening line based on benefits.** Your opening line should capture attention as well as raise the listener's curiosity. The listener should want to hear more. For example, a woman who sells jewelry might say, "I'm Suzanne Smith, and I help women to shine and sparkle." It is not necessary to include your title in your opening line.

▶ **Practice!** Your elevator speech should flow easily. Practice your speech until you come across as confident, sincere, and engaging.

success steps

CREATING AN ELEVATOR SPEECH

1. Consider the benefits that you can deliver.
2. Create a captivating opening line based on benefits.
3. Practice!

4

Having your "elevator speech" prepared and practiced will allow you to create interest in your abilities and provide opportunities for networking in many places.

apply it

Elevator Speech Preparation

GOAL: To prepare an effective elevator speech.

STEP 1: Individually, follow the steps for preparing an elevator speech listed in this chapter. Prepare several introductory statements that are engaging, summarize the benefits of your skills, and stimulate further interest.

STEP 2: After individuals have prepared their elevator speeches, gather in small groups and share your speeches. Share feedback and suggestions for improvement. You may find ways to combine the statements that you have prepared to make an even greater impact.

STEP 3: Practice your elevator speech with a classmate until you can deliver it smoothly and effectively.

THE INFORMATIONAL INTERVIEW

The informational interview is conducted to obtain information about a field or specific company. It is more formal than networking and chance encounters in that it is a scheduled appointment for which you must thoughtfully prepare. The Career Center at Florida State University (2004) and Crosby (2002) list the following purposes of the informational interview:

- to gain information about a career or profession
- to gain information about a specific organization
- to improve your general interviewing skills and ability to communicate with a variety of professionals
- to use as a networking tool to broaden your base of professional contacts
- to gain insight into the realities of the workplace
- to learn effective methods of preparing for a specific career
- to discover new careers and fields that may be of interest

Steps in Informational Interviewing

The steps of an informational interview are similar to preparing for networking opportunities. Research, question preparation, and courteous professional skills are all of paramount importance. Consider the following steps for preparing a productive informational interview, adapted from Crosby (2002):

- **Do your research.** As was the case with networking, effective research will provide you with a strong basis for your interviewing and will allow you to ask more effective questions and acquire more in-depth information. Consider professional organizations, instructors, and the career placement department at your school as sources for your research.
- **Select a person to interview.** Your research sources may also be able to suggest individuals to interview. Consider the following considerations when selecting a person to interview:
  - Select individuals in the field in which you are interested. Crosby points out that these individuals will know more about your field than human resource personnel do.
  - Select individuals who have approximately the same level of responsibility that you would have upon entry into the field.
- **Set up the interview.** Interviews can be arranged by telephone, letter, or e-mail, with a letter being the most common method. If you make contact with a letter or e-mail, follow up with a telephone call. Indicate in the written correspondence that you will be

following up on a specific date and be sure to do so. Include the following information in your request for an informational interview:

▶ If making contact by telephone, ask if this is a good time to talk. If not, arrange a better time.

▶ Provide your name and a brief introduction.

▶ Give the name of the referring person or how you found the individual.

▶ Present your request for a meeting and a brief description of what you hope to accomplish.

▶ Provide information regarding the follow-up telephone call if you are writing a letter.

▶ **Prepare effectively.** Research the organization as thoroughly as possible. Being knowledgeable demonstrates a genuine interest and increases your credibility. Bring your current resume. A general resume may be more effective so that you can revise it based on the outcome of the informational interview. Prepare the questions that you will ask at the interview. Try to ask questions that will help you to gain an understanding of what the job is really like.

▶ **Dress appropriately.** Although less formal than a job interview, the informational interview requires that you present yourself professionally. Chapter 6 discusses professional dressing in depth.

▶ **Pay attention to time frames.** Typically, informational interviews last 20–30 minutes. As with any professional appointment, it is imperative that you arrive on time and respect the time limitations you or your interviewee have set. Effective preparation will allow you to maximize your interview time by having prepared and focused questions.

▶ **Write a thank-you note.** Follow up with a handwritten note expressing your appreciation for the time that the individual spent with you. The note can be brief; it might include appreciation for the time and advice you received along with a summary of the most helpful information. Send the thank-you note within a day or two of the interview.

success steps

INFORMATION INTERVIEWS

1. Do your research.
2. Select a person to interview.
3. Set up the interview.

4. Prepare effectively.
5. Dress appropriately.
6. Pay attention to time frames.
7. Write a thank-you note.

apply it

Informational Interview Preparation

GOAL: To prepare for an effective informational interview.

STEP 1: Prepare a list of individuals in your field whom you would like to interview. Consider those who are employed at an organization in which you are interested. Prepare a brief introduction of yourself and your goal.

STEP 2: Prepare a list of topic-related, open-ended questions that would be appropriately asked during an informational interview. Research "informational interview" on the Internet and look for examples of questions that you might use in your interview.

STEP 3: Practice your interview with a classmate, instructor, or other colleague. Ask these people to critique your performance; set goals to improve based on their feedback.

apply it

Informational Interview Practice

GOAL: To prepare for an effective informational interview.

STEP 1: Prepare a list of individuals in your field whom you would like to interview. Consider those who can offer information about a job in which you are truly interested.

STEP 2: Prepare a list of questions that you would like to ask each individual. Meet with a group of students who are completing this activity and share ideas for effective interviewing questions.

STEP 3: Team up as pairs and practice your informational interviewing skills. Consider making the practice as realistic as possible by dressing professionally and writing a thank-you note.

STEP 4: Throughout the process, provide constructive feedback and suggestions to your interviewing partner.

4

CHAPTER SUMMARY

Networking as a means of developing professional contacts was the main theme of this chapter. You learned what networking is as well as what it is not, and you explored formal and informal networking techniques. Etiquette and follow-up were stressed as important components of the networking process. Variations on networking, such as informational interviews and elevator speeches, were also emphasized.

POINTS TO KEEP IN MIND

In this chapter, several main points were discussed in detail:

- Networking is the establishment and maintenance of mutually supportive professional relationships over time.
- Networking is *not* getting a referral every time you speak to someone.
- Successful networking depends on long-term relationships and giving back to others.
- Networking can serve a variety of purposes, although as a college student your main purpose for networking is likely to be finding employment.
- Networking venues are typically of two types: those that exist and those that you create.
- It is critical to write thank-you notes and express appreciation for assistance.

LEARNING OBJECTIVES REVISITED

Review the learning objectives for this chapter and rate your level of achievement for each objective using the rating scale provided. For each objective on which you do not rate yourself as a 3, outline a plan of action that you will take to fully achieve the objective. Include a time frame for this plan.

1 = did not successfully achieve objective

2 = understand what is needed, but need more study or practice

3 = achieved learning objective thoroughly

	1	2	3
Define *networking* and describe what it is not.	☐	☐	☐
Describe the purposes of networking.	☐	☐	☐
Describe various networking venues and how each is best utilized.	☐	☐	☐
Practice steps of effective networking in various settings.	☐	☐	☐
Implement strategies to increase the effectiveness of networking.	☐	☐	☐
Implement additional networking techniques such as informational interviewing.	☐	☐	☐

Steps to Achieve Unmet Objectives

Steps   Due Date

1. _____   _____

2. _____   _____

3. _____   _____

4. _____   _____

SUGGESTED ITEMS FOR LEARNING PORTFOLIO

▸ Reflection and Critical Thinking Questions: Include your written responses to these questions. Use them to review your development over time.

▸ Networking Plan: This activity will guide you in developing skills for successful networking.

▸ Networking Preparation: Record the outcomes of this activity in your portfolio and update this resource for your networking events and activities as you develop additional questions and gather information.

▸ Networking Simulation: Keep notes from these practice sessions to help you develop your networking skills.

4

▶ Elevator Speech Preparation: Record ideas for your elevator speech. As you use them, keep notes regarding their effectiveness.

▶ Informational Interview Preparation: This activity is intended to prepare you for developing informational interviewing skills that will support your professional development.

▶ Informational Interview Practice: Keep records of your practice sessions and feedback that you receive. Make notes regarding changes that you can make to improve your performance.

REFERENCES

American Association of Retired Persons (n.d.). Networking for a job: What it is and how to do it. Retrieved April 6, 2005, from http://www.aarp.org/money/careers/findingajob/communityresources/a2004-05-10-networkingjob.html

Bguides.com. (2005). The 9 essentials of networking with people and creating more opportunity (2nd ed.). Bguides: Guides to get business done™. Richmond, VA: MaxPitch Media, Inc. Retrieved May 22, 2006, from http://www.bguides.com

The Career Center, Florida State University. (2004). Information interviews. Retrieved April 8, 2005, from http://www.career.fsu.edu/ccis/guides/infoint.html

Crosby, O. (2002, Summer). Informational interviewing: Get the inside scoop on careers [Electronic version]. *Occupational Outlook Quarterly, 46*(2). Bureau of Labor and Statistics. Retrieved April 8, 2005, from http://www.bls.gov/opub/ooq/2002/summer/art03.pdf

Flantzer, H. (n.d.). Networking for career success. Networking for Professionals: The Best in Professional Networking. Retrieved April 4, 2005, from http://www.networkingforprofessionals.com/NFCS.php

Kovar, R. (n.d.(a)). Networking—A key factor in a successful job search. Networking for Professionals: The Best in Professional Networking. Retrieved April 4, 2005, from http://www.networkingforprofessionals.com/NJS.php

Kovar, R. (n.d.(b)). People know people. Networking for Professionals: The Best in Professional Networking. Retrieved April 4, 2005, from http://www.networkingforprofessionals.com/RK.php

Kurow, D. (2002). Preparing your elevator speech. Networking for Professionals: The Best in Professional Networking. Retrieved April 4, 2005, from http://www.networkingforprofessionals.com/DK.php

Welch, T. (n.d.). When you connect with others you move mountains. Networking for Professionals: The Best in Professional Networking. Retrieved April 4, 2005, from http://www.networkingforprofessionals.com/MM.php

Zucker, R. (n.d.). Staying networked. Networking for Professionals: The Best in Professional Networking. Retrieved April 4, 2005, from http://www.networkingforprofessionals.com/SN.php

4

©Digital Vision

CHAPTER OUTLINE

Purpose of the Resume

Types of Resumes

Resume Formats

Guidelines to Creating a Resume

Utilizing Technology to Send Resumes

Cover Letters

References and Recommendations

5 Resume and Cover Letter Development

THE BIG PICTURE

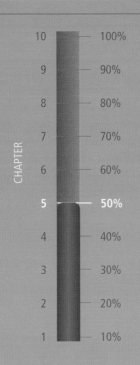

CHAPTER	
10	100%
9	90%
8	80%
7	70%
6	60%
5	**50%**
4	40%
3	30%
2	20%
1	10%

LEARNING OBJECTIVES

By the end of this chapter, you will achieve the following objectives:

▶ Explain the purpose of a resume.
▶ List the elements that are typically required on a resume.
▶ Discuss some general guidelines for preparing a resume.
▶ Compare and contrast the various types of resumes.
▶ Describe the various formats in which resumes can be prepared.
▶ Explain the general guidelines for making a resume scannable.
▶ Discuss how to appropriately e-mail a resume.
▶ Explain how resumes can be entered into Web databases.
▶ Describe how to be cyber-safe.
▶ Demonstrate the ability to write a variety of types of correspondence letters.
▶ Demonstrate the ability to prepare a professional resume.
▶ Demonstrate the ability to prepare a reference sheet.
▶ Demonstrate the ability to write a cover letter.

TOPIC SCENARIO

As a college graduate, Mike Lanham has become very successful in his profession. In his newly acquired position as a manager, Mike's first task is to hire individuals to fill a number of vacant positions within his department. This will be Mike's first experience in hiring. The positions Mike must fill range from highly technical to clerical. To begin the process of hiring, Mike reviews the received resumes. In addition to the technical skills and abilities that are listed, Mike also pays close attention to the appearance of the resume. From the appearance Mike believes he can more easily identify organized individuals.

Based on this short description of Mike's task, answer the following questions:

- How can a resume indicate if an individual is organized, detailed, and professional?
- How much weight should the appearance of a resume carry in the selection process?
- Do you think Mike is being unfair to applicants who do not exhibit these skills through the appearance of their resumes? Should Mike consider these individuals anyway?
- If you have developed a resume, do you think your resume indicates that you are an organized, detailed, and professional individual? If so, how? If not, why not?

PURPOSE OF THE RESUME

The purpose of a resume is to demonstrate to the reader that you are qualified or have the appropriate skills for a position. The goal of submitting a resume is to lead to an interview. Because employers have many responsibilities and limited time, applicants need to understand that resumes must say a lot in a very short and concise manner. Typically, an employer will spend no more than 30 seconds reviewing a resume. Within those 30 seconds, resumes can be either thrown aside or kept for further review.

The resume should be a statement summarizing your abilities, skills, and professionalism. The words and appearance provide the employer with a first impression of the applicant.

The National Association of Colleges and Employers (n.d.) suggests the following general guidelines for preparing a resume:

- **Know your skills and abilities.** Take a self-assessment test in order to be clear on what you can offer future employers.
- **Have your information outlined prior to writing your resume.** Outlining your skills, abilities, and work experience will simplify the task of writing your resume.

Employers may receive hundreds of resumes for one position and will spend a minimal amount of time reviewing each. Make sure your resume is professional in its appearance and conveys your skills and abilities at a glance.

▶ **Be clear on the position for which you are applying.** Review your resume prior to each submission to ensure that you are providing information relevant to the position.

▶ **Utilize appropriate tools to give your resume a professional appearance.** Paper size, paper weight, envelope size, and strength of ink are elements to consider.

▶ **Choose an appropriate resume for the job.** Be clear on what type of resume will work best for the job you are applying for.

success steps

PREPARING TO WRITE A RESUME

1. Know your skills and abilities.
2. Have your information outlined prior to writing your resume.
3. Be clear on the position for which you are applying.
4. Utilize appropriate tools to give your resume a professional appearance.
5. Choose an appropriate resume for the job.

▶ **REFLECTION QUESTIONS**

- How thorough is your knowledge regarding preparation of a resume?
- What else would you like to learn about the process of resume writing?

? CRITICAL THINKING QUESTION

5–1. How can you determine if a resume contains enough material, too much, or too little?

TYPES OF RESUMES

There are a variety of different resumes from which individuals can choose. These include:

▶ chronological resume

▶ functional resume

▶ combination resume

▶ curriculum vitae

The choice of resume type depends on the applicant's experience and the amount of information the employer is seeking.

THE CHRONOLOGICAL RESUME

The chronological resume lists professional experience in reverse chronological order. Chronological resumes are typically preferred by employers because they are perceived as fact based and can be easily reviewed. Due to its format, the chronological resume works best for individuals with "solid experience and a logical job history" (JobStar Central, 2006(a)). Those who have experienced career changes and lack experience may find the chronological resume more difficult to use. Figure 5–1 is an example of the chronological resume.

Resume Sample: Chronological Format

Jesse Three Crows
23 First Street ■ Albany, NY 12208
(518) 555-3647 ■ jthreecrows@aol.com

WORK EXPERIENCE:

September 2002 to Present	Assistant Bookkeeper, Achievement Office Sales/Service, Albany, NY. Aid in bookkeeping, payroll services, and tax preparation.
September 2003 to May 2004	Internship at Goldworthy & Ames Certified Public Accountants, Albany, NY. Provided tax preparation assistance for five major clients.
September 2001 to April 2002	Tutor, Teaching and Learning Center, The College of Saint Rose, Albany, NY. Provided tutoring assistance in Math 121, 122 and Statistics I and II to students on an individual basis.
May 2000 to September 2004	Groundskeeper. Albany High School, Albany, NY. Maintained school grounds during summer break.

EDUCATION:

September 2000 to May 2004	The College of Saint Rose, Albany, NY Bachelor of Science degree in Business Administration conferred in May 2004 Accounting GPA: 3.8 Overall GPA: 3.5
COMPUTER SKILLS:	Microsoft Office and Apple applications
LEADERSHIP EXPERIENCES:	Supervisor and team leader of client audits Co-captain 1999–2000 State Championship basketball team. Two gold medals and one bronze–Team Handball–Empire State Games
REFERENCES:	Available upon request.

FIGURE 5–1.   A chronological resume lists the applicant's experience in the order in which it occurred.

THE FUNCTIONAL RESUME

The functional resume lists experience by type rather than chronologically. For example (as also discussed in Chapter 3 in the context of portfolios), on a functional resume management experience from several positions would be grouped in one section. Computer skills would be grouped in another. Some employers may feel that the functional resume is more difficult to review, as it is less structured than a chronological resume and it is more difficult to associate experience with a specific job.

JobStar Central (2006(b)) states that the functional resume works best for those individuals

▶ whose work history is varied, with no clear career link between each job

▶ who are new college graduates entering the workforce with little work experience

▶ whose past job titles do not clearly indicate the level of skills used

▶ who are trying to make a career change

Figure 5–2 illustrates the functional resume.

Resume Sample: Functional Format

Jesse Three Crows
23 First Street ■ Albany, NY 12208
(518) 555-3647 ■ jthreecrows@aol.com

SKILLS / ACHIEVEMENTS: Supervisor and team leader of client audits.

Excellent computer skills, including Microsoft Office and Apple applications.

Working with clients and interpreting their needs.

Working under the pressure of deadlines.

EMPLOYMENT HISTORY: Assistant Bookkeeper, Achievement Office Sales/Service, Albany, NY. 2002 to present.

Intern, Goldworthy & Ames Certified Public Accountants, Albany, NY. 2003 to 2004.

Tutor, Teaching and Learning Center, The College of Saint Rose, Albany, NY. 2001 to 2002.

Groundskeeper, Albany High School, Albany, NY. 2000 to 2004.

EDUCATION: Bachelor of Science degree, Business Administration, The College of Saint Rose, Albany, NY, May 2004.

RELEVANT COURSES: Financial Accounting, Behavioral Science in Business, Urban Economics, Managerial Economics, Financial Information Systems, Taxation, Strategic Marketing Planning, Investment Theory, New Business Ventures and the Entrepreneur, Performance and Financial Auditing.

REFERENCES: Available upon request.

FIGURE 5–2.   A functional resume presents the applicant's experience by type.

COMBINATION RESUMES

A combination resume blends features of both chronological and functional resumes. Figure 5–3 is an example of a combination resume.

Resume Sample: Combination Format

Jesse Three Crows
23 First Street ■ Albany, NY 12208
(518) 555-3647 ■ jthreecrows@aol.com

SKILLS / ACHIEVEMENTS:

Supervisor and team leader of client audits.

Excellent computer skills, including Microsoft Office and Apple applications.

Working with clients and interpreting their needs.

Working under the pressure of deadlines.

WORK EXPERIENCE:

September 2002 to Present — Assistant Bookkeeper, Achievement Office Sales/Service, Albany, NY. Aid in bookkeeping, payroll services, and tax preparation.

September 2003 to May 2004 — Internship at Goldworthy & Ames Certified Public Accountants, Albany, NY. Provided tax preparation assistance for five major clients.

September 2001 to April 2002 — Tutor, Teaching and Learning Center, The College of Saint Rose, Albany, NY. Provided tutoring assistance in Math 121, 122 and Statistics I and II to students on an individual basis.

May 2000 to September 2004 — Groundskeeper. Albany High School, Albany, NY. Maintained school grounds during summer break.

EDUCATION:

September 2000 to May 2004 — The College of Saint Rose, Albany, NY
Bachelor of Science degree in Business Administration conferred in May 2004
Accounting GPA: 3.8
Overall GPA: 3.5

REFERENCES:

Available upon request.

FIGURE 5–3. A combination resume uses features of both the chronological and functional resumes.

THE CURRICULUM VITAE

Depending on the profession, the curriculum vitae may be most appropriate. The curriculum vitae (CV) is a detailed description of all academic and professional pursuits, including educational endeavors, professional positions and their related duties, publications, presentations given and attended, volunteer work, organizational memberships and positions held, and honors and recognition that have been received. While the chronological or functional resume is no more than one or two pages, a curriculum vitae can be 15–20 pages. The CV is most commonly used in academic and research settings. The detail of a CV makes it appropriate mainly for individuals who have extensive experience and credentials.

RESUME FORMATS

Resume formats will depend on your field and the requirements of the employer. Consider the following formats.

ELECTRONIC RESUMES

An electronic resume is intended to be delivered via e-mail or through an online application form. The electronic resume has no text formatting, making it scannable, or able to be read by any e-mail or resume tracking program. For example, using all capital letters in a standard font such as Times or Helvetica for headings eliminates formatting that might be specific to your word processing program.

The following guidelines to facilitate electronic processing of a resume are suggested by Seneca College of Applied Arts and Technology Career Services (2001) and The Santa Clara University Career Center (n.d.):

- Use plain fonts, such as Arial, Verdana, Helvetica, or Courier.
- Do not use italics, boldface, or underlined text.
- Use 10- or 12-point font.
- Do not use graphics, decorative borders, or other visual elements.
- Avoid using indentations to minimize the problem of misalignment and document asymmetry. Separate sections using capitalized headings and an additional line of space.
- Adjust margins so that the resume fits into a standard e-mail window. The left margin should be set at 1 inch and the right margin at 3 inches.

▶ Save your document as "Text Only with Line Breaks." Your word processing program may warn you that you will be losing some of the formatting. Click "OK."

▶ Edit and clean up your document by opening it in a text editor program such as Notepad®.

▶ Use a bulleted list to present information clearly and concisely.

▶ Cut and paste your resume into the body of an e-mail rather than sending it as an attachment.

▶ Conduct a trial run by sending the resume to a friend with a different e-mail program to test its legibility. Ask the friend to print the document to ensure that it prints accurately.

WEB RESUMES

A Web resume is posted on the Internet and is typically used to display an individual's skills in designing hypertext markup language (HTML) documents. It is beneficial to individuals seeking art or graphics positions and has the capacity to include electronic media such as video, audio, and advanced graphics.

SELECTING A RESUME FORMAT

Experts recommend keeping copies of your resume in various formats so that you will be prepared to respond to a specific employer's request. Dikel (2004) recommends the following formats:

▶ A printable version completed in a word processing program that can be printed and mailed in hard copy. A printable version of your resume can include elements such as boldface type, bullets, and graphics.

▶ A plaintext (ASCII) version appropriate for pasting into online forms. This version follows the guidelines for an electronic resume.

▶ An e-mail version (also ASCII) that is formatted for the length-of-line restrictions in e-mail and meets the requirements for an electronic resume.

GUIDELINES TO CREATING A RESUME

Regardless of the resume format, employers typically need similar information. Include the following information on the resume, not necessarily in

▶ REFLECTION QUESTIONS

• With which of the resume formats are you familiar? With which would you like to become more familiar?

• If you have an existing resume, how do you think your chosen format has served you in the past? If it has been effective, why? If not, why not?

? CRITICAL THINKING QUESTION

5–2. What is your reaction to the following statement? "Since it takes a lot of extra work to create various versions of the resume, I don't think that is necessary."

5

this order (Hess, 1999):

- contact information, including name, address, telephone number, and e-mail address
- summary of qualifications
- education, including names and locations of schools, dates attended and date of graduation, major course of study, and degree earned
- work history (paid experience)
- volunteer work history (unpaid experience)
- specialty certifications, credentials, or licenses
- military experience
- professional memberships and positions held
- information regarding special skills, recognition, and achievements

The following are some simple guidelines to follow when compiling your resume:

- **Customize your resume.** A resume targeted at a specific job is most effective. Customize your resume so that your skills and achievements support the job for which you are applying. This does mean that you will need to adjust your resume each time you apply for a job, but better results are worth that extra effort.

- **Be prepared with the information you need to write your resume.** Collect all pertinent information such as job history, transcripts, certifications, and other documents that contain data that you will include on your resume. This eliminates or minimizes the need to search for information and will make more efficient use of your time.

- **Select the best resume type for your needs.** Be clear on which resume type is the best choice for effectively presenting your information relative to the job requirements. Make sure to check if an electronic resume is required.

- **Use available resources to help with the composition of your resume.** There are a variety of resources that provide sample copies and suggestions for resumes. Conduct an Internet search using "resumes" or "resume writing" as your search term. Also, seek assistance from the career center on your campus.

- **Consider additions to your resume based on your field.** Depending on the job for which you are applying, additions to the resume can be helpful. For example, in the graphic arts field, added visual interest can demonstrate creativity. Follow the standards of your field. Whatever you add should be simple and professional. Your words should be the focus.

5

5

? CRITICAL THINKING QUESTIONS

5–3. What other action verbs can you think of? Compile a list and refer to it when writing your resume.

5–4. Which action verbs are most appropriate for your field and experience?

▶ **Limit the length of functional or chronological resumes.** A length of one or two pages is ideal. Pages should be added only if they are absolutely necessary to effectively represent your experience.

▶ **Use bullets for an easy read.** Avoid using long sentences and being too wordy. Use phrases that convey your points clearly and concisely.

▶ **Use action verbs and phrases to describe your accomplishments and skills.** Select words that convey precise and efficient action when describing your accomplishments. According to Barthel and Goldrick-Jones (n.d., "Consider Word Choice Carefully"), your resume should "sound positive and confident; neither too aggressive, nor overly modest." Examples of action verbs include *created, modified, directed, supervised, wrote, illustrated,* and *managed*.

▶ **Use a professional tone.** Avoid extensive use of pronouns such as "I" or "me," especially at the beginning of paragraphs. Write in a formal conversational tone. Avoid contractions (use "do not" instead of "don't") and avoid abbreviations and slang.

▶ **Use a professional e-mail address.** E-mail addresses that are used socially, intended to be fun and amusing, may not be appropriate for professional correspondence. Thoughtfully consider your e-mail address. If it in any way presents an unprofessional image or can be interpreted as offensive, consider creating another account for professional use. Your Internet service provider (ISP) may offer additional mailboxes with your subscription or you may use one of the free services offered on the Internet. A professional e-mail would be your name or a variation on it. An example is susan.smith@yourISP.com.

▶ **Include all important information that employers will want.** For example, a job history must include the name of the employer, your job title, job location, and dates of employment. Reasons for leaving a job should not be included.

▶ **Check for accuracy.** Make sure your address, phone numbers, and e-mail address are correct. Use only permanent addresses. Ensure that your outgoing voice mail message is professional and appropriate for an employer to hear.

▶ **Represent well-rounded skills.** Include both technical and soft skills on your resume.

▶ **Use discretion with personal interests.** Personal hobbies and activities should not be listed unless they are related to the job you are seeking.

▶ **Be honest about your abilities.** Never embellish your experience or skills. You do not want to mislead employers to assume you are more qualified than you actually are.

▶ **Include only postsecondary experience.** As a college graduate, list only your college experience. High school graduation should not be listed.

▶ **Do not list personal information on your resume.** Information pertaining to religion, marital status, and ethnicity should not be listed on the resume.

▶ **Limit lengthy experience.** If your work experience spans more than 10 years, it is acceptable to list the most recent 10 years only. List more only if the experience relates directly to the job.

▶ **Pay attention to mechanics.** Make sure your resume is professional by paying close attention to spacing, spelling, and grammar. Barthel and Goldrick-Jones (n.d., "Evaluate Your Resume") suggest that you assess the appearance of your resume and ask the following questions:

  ▶ Is the page too busy with different type styles, sizes, lines, or boxes?

  ▶ Is there too much white space? (White space is the area on the resume that does not contain any writing or graphics.) White space should be sufficient to allow easy reading, but not so much that the content appears sparse.

  ▶ Is important information quick and easy to find?

▶ **Get a professional opinion.** Ask a professional, such as the personnel in your campus career center or a colleague in the field, to review your resume. Be open to constructive criticism. You want your resume to be the best it can be.

▶ **Include a thoughtful career objective.** Include a career objective that is stated as a goal and reflects the characteristics of the position you are seeking. An example of a career objective is "Seeking a position as a medical assistant in a medium-size family practice." The career objective is placed at the beginning of the resume, following your contact information.

▶ **Check for legibility.** If providing a hard copy to the employer, make sure the printed copy of your resume is easy to read and that the paper is of good quality. High-quality white paper is the most appropriate.

▶ **List references separately.** Speak to people who know you and your work about being a reference for you. List them on a separate reference sheet.

REFLECTION QUESTIONS

- What did you learn from the resume guidelines?
- If you have an existing resume, how might your resume change based on what you have learned from the guidelines?

? CRITICAL THINKING QUESTION

5–5. Do you think it is important to follow these guidelines or do you think more individuality should be allowed when it comes to content and style on one's resume?

©Digital Vision

Today, resumes are commonly sent via e-mail or posted on the Internet. Remember that in some situations, however, it is a good practice to also send a hard copy via surface mail.

success steps

COMPLETING A RESUME

1. Be prepared with the information you need prior to writing your resume.
2. Select the best resume type for your needs.
3. Use resources on the Internet to help with the composition of your resume.
4. Consider additions to your resume based on your field.
5. Try to limit functional or chronological resumes to one page.
6. Use bullets for an easy read.
7. Use action verbs and phrases to describe your accomplishments and skills.
8. Use a professional tone.
9. Don't leave out important information that employers will want.
10. Check for accuracy.
11. Represent well-rounded skills.
12. Use discretion about including personal interests.
13. Be honest about your abilities.
14. Include only postsecondary experience.
15. Do not list personal information on your resume.
16. Limit lengthy experience.
17. Pay attention to mechanics.
18. Check for legibility.
19. List references separately.

UTILIZING TECHNOLOGY TO SEND RESUMES

In addition to the more traditional methods of mailing and faxing, e-mailing or posting a resume on the Internet have become common practice today. Using these methods requires only a slight change to the format of the resume.

SENDING RESUMES VIA E-MAIL

The following are guidelines to follow when e-mailing a resume (Minnesota Department of Employment and Economic Development, 1994–2004):

▶ Usually, unsolicited resumes should not be sent by e-mail.

▶ Conducting mass e-mailings of your resume is not an effective marketing tool.

▶ After e-mailing your resume, follow up with a phone call.

▶ It is recommended that you send a hard copy in the mail. Indicate in your original e-mail that you have also mailed a hard copy.

▶ Be sure that the employer can receive attachments if you are including attachments.

▶ Be sure that the employer has the correct software version to receive your resume.

▶ Always include a cover letter with your e-mailed resume.

▶ Address your cover letter to a specific person. Avoid using the phrase "To whom it may concern."

POSTING RESUMES ON THE WEB

Entering the resume into a job database is another way to respond to a job opportunity. Today, there are job search sites and placement services where resumes can be posted and are available to employers. The following are typical steps for displaying a resume on a Web database, based on criteria from Seneca College Career Services (2001):

1. Register with the Web site, by providing
   ▶ contact information, including name, address, e-mail address, and so forth.
   ▶ other demographic information that is requested.
2. Follow the instructions for setting up a password.
3. Register for e-mail services, such as job alerts.
4. Post your resume.

Displaying the resume on your own Web site is also an option. It is easier to upload the resume to a Web site if certain composition elements have been considered. Choose one of the following alternatives for simplifying the upload process (Seneca College Career Services, 2001):

▶ Compose the resume in Notepad or another text editor and manually encode it using HTML.

▶ Create the resume in Microsoft Word® and save it as HTML.

▶ Prepare the resume using a Web page authoring tool that is part of your Web browser, such as Netscape Composer.

▶ Format the resume using Web page authoring software, like Dreamweaver® or ColdFusion®.

It is relatively easy to post a resume on a Web site. Many Internet service providers (ISPs) offer a personal home page with a subscription to the

5

service. If this is not available from the ISP as part of a subscription, space can be rented.

SAFETY ON THE WEB

With the growing use of Internet technologies, individuals need to take some precautions to remain cyber-safe. The following are some safety considerations recommended by Dikel (2004):

▶ **Limit where you post your resume on the Internet.** Avoid "over-posting." Limit your postings to three or four job sites.

▶ **Pay attention to privacy policies.** Ensure that your personal information will not be released without your knowledge.

▶ **Expect a trial period.** Use sites that allow you to view and evaluate the usefulness of the site before making a long-term commitment.

▶ **Carefully consider your contact information.** Be wise about how much contact information you provide. For example, consider only providing e-mail information rather than your name, address, and phone numbers.

▶ **Give general information.** Use general information and descriptions to present employment history. Avoid using company names and dates of employment.

▶ **Keep information current.** Repost your resume every 14 days so that it appears as a fresh submission. If a response is not received in a month or so, remove it and find another posting site.

▶ **Remove promptly when appropriate.** Once you are hired, delete all posted resumes.

REFLECTION QUESTION

- What concerns might you have regarding the use of some of these more advanced methods for sending your resume? What might you do to overcome these concerns?

? CRITICAL THINKING QUESTION

5–6. How might technology continue to change how resumes are sent to employers?

success steps

BEING CYBER-SAFE

1. Limit where you post your resume on the Internet.
2. Pay attention to privacy policies.
3. Expect a trial period.
4. Carefully consider your contact information.
5. Give general information.
6. Keep information current.
7. Remove your resume promptly when appropriate.

apply it

Utilizing Technology to Send Resumes

GOAL: *To develop a clearer understanding of how to use technology to send resumes.*

STEP 1: Conduct research on the Web to further understand how technology can be used to send your resume.

STEP 2: If technology is not your strength, schedule a meeting with someone who is more knowledgeable in this area to help clarify areas that are unclear.

STEP 3: Write a report of your findings and what you learned.

STEP 4: Consider placing this report in your Learning Portfolio.

COVER LETTERS

The cover letter is a tool for introducing yourself to an employer and is a required element when submitting a resume. The cover letter provides the opportunity to give additional information regarding your skills and experience and to summarize how they relate to the desired job. The cover letter should clearly convey what you have to offer to the employer. Do not focus on yourself; avoid statements such as, "this would be a great opportunity for me." The cover letter should not exceed one page in length. Princeton University Career Services (n.d.) provides the following general guidelines to consider when developing a cover letter:

▶ Each cover letter should be written in response to the specific job requirements. Sending a generic cover letter is strongly discouraged.

▶ Keep copies of all cover letters in order to refer back to as needed.

▶ The cover letter must provide information that clearly illustrates how your skills and experiences match what the organization is seeking.

▶ Whenever possible, cover letters should be addressed to a specific person.

▶ If the job comes through a referral, mention this in the cover letter. Include this information in the opening paragraph. A familiar name is more likely to capture and hold the interest of the reader.

▶ Professionalism in the cover letter is as critical as in the resume. Pay attention to elements such as spelling, grammar, spacing, professional tone, and paper quality. Elements of the cover letter should match those in the resume.

A well-written cover letter can provide the prospective employer with information about an applicant's personality, ability for being detailed, communication skills, enthusiasm, and intelligence.

The cover letter can also provide the prospective employer a glimpse into who the applicant is as an individual.

The Writing Center at Rensselaer Polytechnic Institute (n.d.) recommends that the format of the cover letter include the following:

- Paragraphs should reflect a formal conversational tone.
- The first paragraph usually is brief and tells which job you are applying for as well as where you learned about the position.
- The body of the letter can range from one to three paragraphs. These paragraphs provide the opportunity to elaborate on your qualifications and experiences. Being specific regarding how these abilities and experiences match well with the desired job is critical.
- The last paragraph contains a request for further contact and states how this contact can be achieved.

Figure 5–4 shows a sample cover letter.

William Running Deer
432 East Brooks Avenue
Denver, CO 80000

November 3, 2005

Ms. Christina Chung
Human Resources Director
Everett Technologies
10067 Mountain View Road
Broomfield, CO 82222

Dear Ms. Chung:

Enclosed please find my resume in support of my interest in the office manager position that was advertised in the October 30, 2005 edition of the *Denver Gazette* and posted on Everett Technologies' Web site.

The experience that I would bring to Everett Technologies includes a background as an assistant office manager, overseeing the streamlining of various office procedures, and implementing data tracking systems. My qualifications effectively support your stated company goal of developing and putting into practice a new client data management system.

I would very much like to discuss ways in which my experience could contribute to a smooth and efficient transition to a new system and would value the opportunity to further explore how I might support your efforts in the office manager position. Thank you for your consideration and I look forward to hearing from you.

Sincerely,

William Running Deer

FIGURE 5–4.   An effective cover letter provides the employers with a concise yet clear overview of your skills and goals.

apply it

Job Search Materials

GOAL: *To demonstrate the ability to develop a resume, cover letter, and reference sheet.*

STEP 1: Use the information from this chapter and other available resources to develop a resume, cover letter, and reference sheet.

STEP 2: Share your resume with a respected professional and ask for constructive criticism.

STEP 3: Redo areas as instructed by the reviewer and submit to the instructor for review.

STEP 4: Consider putting this project in your Learning Portfolio.

OTHER TYPES OF CORRESPONDENCE

There are other types of correspondence frequently utilized by the job seeker. These include:

- thank-you letters sent following phone or in-person interviews
- letters of inquiry sent to request more information regarding job opportunities or a specific advertised position
- letters requesting withdrawal of one's application
- acceptance letters to indicate acceptance of an offer
- letters to decline an offer
- e-mail correspondence

As with the cover letter, these letters continue to represent the applicant's professionalism. The same attention given to the cover letter should be given to any of these types of correspondence. Various resources, such as the Internet, provide a wealth of information to help individuals produce each of these types of correspondence.

REFERENCES AND RECOMMENDATIONS

Employers usually request the names of individuals who are familiar with your professional performance and will attest to your skills, abilities, and overall professionalism. Include the name, title, address, phone number, and

> **REFLECTION QUESTION**
>
> - How effective are your professional letters? Where might you go for help in developing these skills?

> **? CRITICAL THINKING QUESTION**
>
> 5–7. What is your reaction to the following statement? "A generic cover letter is sufficient, as writing a customized letter for each potential job is too time-consuming."

5

5

e-mail address of each reference. List the elements of each reference on separate lines, as you would when addressing an envelope. Michigan State University Career Development Center (1996) makes the following suggestions for locating individuals who will consent to being listed as references and provide positive recommendations:

▶ Never list an individual who has not given you permission to be listed as a reference. It is critical that you contact and request permission from each person you wish to use as a reference.

▶ Be sure that individuals you list as references can match your experience with the job for which you are applying. Prepare them for questions that they may be asked.

▶ Make sure that the information offered by each reference will place you in the best possible light. Ask each reference directly if he or she will provide a positive recommendation. If someone asks not be used as a reference, respect his or her wishes and substitute someone else.

▶ References must have good communication abilities. Choose references wisely and select those who are able to present themselves professionally.

▶ Send your selected references a copy of your resume. This will assist them in discussing your background and answering questions posed by the employer.

▶ Avoid using photocopies when sending recommendation letters.

▶ Make sure the letters contain all the necessary information the employer will need to contact the reference. Check the address and phone numbers for accuracy.

▶ Letters of recommendations are usually offered to the employer separately from the resume and cover letter package. Providing too much material at the beginning might overwhelm the employer.

▶ Stay in touch with your references during your job search. It is professional and courteous to keep them up to date regarding the jobs for which you are applying, as well as the outcome of each application.

▶ Always thank your references as they provide recommendations for you. Follow up with a telephone call and personally thank them. Sending a handwritten thank-you note is also appropriate.

▶ REFLECTION QUESTIONS

• What individuals would you use as references? Why did you select these individuals? How will they present you in the best possible light?

• What concerns might you have about finding references? How can you effectively address these concerns?

? CRITICAL THINKING QUESTION

5–8. What specific questions might you ask an individual who you are considering using as a reference?

▸ Provide references on a sheet separate from your resume. Select quality paper and use a full sheet. It is typical to list three to eight references, depending on the employer's request. Review your reference list to ensure that its appearance is neat and clean. Include your name and personal contact information on the top of the sheet in case it is separated from your resume.

apply it

Preparing Professional Correspondence

GOAL: To demonstrate the ability to develop a variety of letters used to correspond during the job search.

STEP 1: The instructor should divide the class into two groups. Each group should be given at least three different types of correspondence letters.

STEP 2: Each group should conduct research regarding group members' letters and the appropriate content, layout, and purpose of each. A short report on these findings should be compiled by the group and presented to the class. Handouts or overheads should be encouraged.

STEP 3: Each group member must also write one letter of each type he or she has researched. These are to be turned in to the instructor for review.

STEP 4: Consider putting the correspondence examples from this activity in your Learning Portfolio.

5

CHAPTER SUMMARY

This chapter provided the foundations for preparing a resume, cover letter, and other types of professional correspondence used during the job search process. You learned how to select content for each type of correspondence, as well as how to present it professionally and effectively. Various formats for submitting resumes were reviewed, and you received guidelines for selecting the most appropriate format for your needs.

POINTS TO KEEP IN MIND

In this chapter, several main points were discussed in detail:

- ▶ The purpose of a resume is to spark an interest with the potential employer by pointing out your abilities, skills, and professionalism.
- ▶ Resumes must be short, concise, yet full of details.
- ▶ Resume types include chronological, functional, combination, and the curriculum vitae.
- ▶ Recent college graduates typically choose to use either the functional or combination resume.
- ▶ Various formats of resumes include printed, scannable, plaintext, e-mail, and Web versions.
- ▶ Standard guidelines for creating a resume include using bullets for an easier read, avoiding long sentences and wordiness, and using action verbs and phrases to describe your accomplishments and skills.
- ▶ Items that should not be included on your resume include use of personal pronouns, temporary addresses and phone numbers, and lists of personal hobbies and activities that are unrelated to the job.
- ▶ Your resume can be sent to an employer in several ways, ranging from traditional methods such as mailing and faxing to more contemporary methods such as e-mailing or posting on the Internet.
- ▶ The cover letter, which must always accompany the resume, should provide further details regarding your skills and experience and how these directly relate to the desired job.
- ▶ Other types of correspondence you may utilize include thank-you letters, letters of inquiry, letters of withdrawal, acceptance letters, letters to decline an offer, and e-mail.
- ▶ References need to be individuals who offer a positive recommendation, present your skills effectively, and exhibit good overall communication skills.

LEARNING OBJECTIVES REVISITED

Review the learning objectives for this chapter and rate your level of achievement for each objective using the rating scale provided. For each objective on which you do not rate yourself as a 3, outline a plan of action that you will take to fully achieve the objective. Include a time frame for this plan.

1 = did not successfully achieve objective

2 = understand what is needed, but need more study or practice

3 = achieved learning objective thoroughly

	1	2	3
List the elements that are typically required on a resume.	☐	☐	☐
Explain the purpose of a resume.	☐	☐	☐
Discuss some general guidelines for preparing a resume.	☐	☐	☐
Compare and contrast the various types of resumes.	☐	☐	☐
Describe the various formats that resumes can be prepared.	☐	☐	☐
Explain the general guidelines for making a resume scannable.	☐	☐	☐
Discuss how to appropriately e-mail a resume.	☐	☐	☐
Explain how resumes can be entered into Web site databases.	☐	☐	☐
Understand how to be more cyber-safe.	☐	☐	☐
Demonstrate the ability to write a variety of types of correspondence letters.	☐	☐	☐
Demonstrate the ability to prepare a professional resume.	☐	☐	☐
Demonstrate the ability to prepare a reference sheet.	☐	☐	☐
Demonstrate the ability to write a cover letter.	☐	☐	☐

Steps to Achieve Unmet Objectives

Steps   Due Date

1. _____   _____

2. _____   _____

3. _____   _____

4. _____   _____

SUGGESTED ITEMS FOR LEARNING PORTFOLIO

▶ Utilizing Technology to Send Resumes: This activity is intended to help you develop a clearer understanding of how to use technology to send resumes.

▌ Job Search Materials: By completing this activity, you will gain experience in developing a resume, cover letter, and reference sheet.

▌ Preparing Professional Correspondence: The goal of this activity is to provide practice in creating a variety of letters used to correspond during the job search.

REFERENCES

Barthel, B. & Goldrick-Jones, A. (n.d.). Resumes [Electronic version]. The Writing Center at Rensselaer Polytechnic Institute. Retrieved March 15, 2005, from http://www.rpi.edu/web/writingcenter/resume.html

Dikel, M. F. (2004). Prepare your resume for emailing or posting on the Internet. Retrieved March 15, 2005, from http://www.rileyguide.com/eresume.html

Hess, P. M. (1999). *Career Success: Right Here Right Now!* (pp. 80–85). Thomson Delmar Learning: Clifton Park, NY.

JobStar Central. (2006(a)). What is the right resume for me? Chronological. Retrieved May 26, 2006, from http://jobstar.org/tools/resume/res-chro.cfm

JobStar Central. (2006(b)). What is the right resume for me? Functional. Retrieved May 26, 2006, from http://jobstar.org/tools/resume/res-func.cfm

Minnesota Department of Employment and Economic Development. (1994–2005). Internet job search strategies—The electronic resume. Retrieved March 18, 2005, from http://www.deed.state.mn.us/cjs/cjsbook/internet3.htm

Michigan State University, Career Development Center. (1996). Establishing references: A guide for jobseekers. Retrieved March 18, 2005, from http://www.msu.edu/user/leedyjen/reflet.htm

National Association of Colleges and Employers. (n.d.). Your guide to resume writing. Retrieved March 15, 2005, from http://www.jobweb.com/Resumes_Interviews/resume_guide/how_to.htm

Princeton University Career Services. (n.d.). Resume guide. Retrieved March 15, 2005, from http://web.princeton.edu/sites/career/Undergrad/JobSearch/resume_guide.html

The Santa Clara University Career Center. (n.d.). Resumes. Retrieved November 3, 2005, from http://www.scu.edu/careercenter/resources/publications/resumes.pdf

Seneca College of Applied Arts and Technology, Career Services. (2001). Using the Internet to apply for jobs. Retrieved March 18, 2005, from http://ilearn.senecac.on.ca/careers/apply/resume/e_resume.html

The Writing Center at Rensselaer Polytechnic Institute. (n.d.). Cover letters. Retrieved March 15, 2005, from http://www.rpi.edu/web/writingcenter/cover_letter.html

5

©Digital Vision

CHAPTER OUTLINE

First Impressions

Dressing for Success

Dressing for the Interview

Building a Professional Wardrobe on a Budget

6 Dressing for Success

THE BIG PICTURE

CHAPTER

10	100%
9	90%
8	80%
7	70%
6	**60%**
5	50%
4	40%
3	30%
2	20%
1	10%

LEARNING OBJECTIVES

By the end of this chapter, you will achieve the following objectives:

▶ Describe appropriate clothing to be worn to an interview.

▶ Understand how first impressions can affect the opinions of others.

▶ Explain how appearance can be improved by paying attention to dressing for body type and skin tone.

▶ Explain how outward appearance can affect internal confidence.

▶ Discuss considerations that should be given to interviewing attire.

▶ Discuss grooming tips that are important to adhere to as a professional.

TOPIC SCENARIO

Jim has always prided himself on demonstrating his individuality through his clothing and general appearance. Jim's clothing style has always been one that involves a variety of colorful items. His favorite outfit consists of loose-fitting denim jeans, a bright green shirt, and boat shoes with no socks. Jim also shows his personality via his long dreadlocks, one earring, and a tattoo on his forearm. Jim strongly believes that these items demonstrate his individualism and are important for others to accept. As a recent college graduate, Jim has been called for his first job interview. In reviewing his wardrobe, Jim begins to select items that he thinks will be appropriate for the interview. Knowing he is uncomfortable in a tie, and does not even own one, Jim decides not to wear a tie. In considering comfort, Jim also decides not to purchase other shoes but to stay with the boat shoes. He does conclude that he should wear socks. Jim decides that other necessary purchases include one pair of casual black pants and a loose-fitting yellow dress shirt. The weather is warm, so Jim decides long sleeves and a jacket are out.

Based on this short description of Jim's interviewing attire, answer the following questions:

▶ Do you think that Jim should be allowed to demonstrate his individualism through his choice of attire for the interview? If not, why not? If so, what do you think is appropriate? Would your answer change if you knew what type of job Jim was applying for? If so, how and why?

▶ Other than Jim's clothing issues, what other areas of Jim's appearance should he consider?

▶ If you were interviewing Jim, would you have any objections to Jim wearing short sleeves? Would the tattoo or earring be an issue? Why or why not?

▶ If Jim was an African American, do you think it would be more appropriate for him to wear dreadlocks than for a Caucasian male? If so, why?

▶ Would Jim be wise to change his hairstyle for the interview?

▶ What is your best advice to Jim regarding his wardrobe and appearance?

▶ Do you think employers pay too much attention to appearance and clothing? Explain your answer.

©Digital Vision

Casual and comfortable dress may be fine for campus life, but to make a positive first impression on potential employers, professional attire is a must. Casual campus dress such as that in the picture is not appropriate for an interview.

6

FIRST IMPRESSIONS

When pursuing a job, it is important to recognize the critical nature of making a good first impression. First impressions begin as soon as contact is made with a company of interest. This contact can occur through either written or spoken communication. Impressions are made through your resume, cover letter, and initial phone call; at the moment you visit to pick up an application; when you walk in for the interview; and when the first and subsequent interviews occur. During all these times the applicant is being scrutinized and evaluated. Conclusions are being drawn about one's professionalism and personality based on appearance, mannerisms, communication style, attitude, confidence level, and social skills.

Although some individuals may not like the idea that they are being judged by their appearance, it is important to accept that

- ◗ dress and grooming are important and are a critical factor in getting hired.
- ◗ first impressions do matter.
- ◗ overall dress does affect one's professional success.

Given these facts, it is critical for those who seek success both in obtaining a job and advancing in their careers to work toward improving their fashion sense, style, and grooming habits.

---

success tips

DRESSING TO MAKE A GOOD IMPRESSION

1. Remember that dress and grooming are both critical factors in getting hired.
2. Keep in mind that first impressions *do* matter.
3. Accept that overall dressing and grooming habits have an impact on professional success.

Understanding and accepting that your personal appearance does make a difference is the first step in presenting yourself effectively to potential employers. Developing the skills and presentation necessary to make a good impression is the second step and will be what differentiates a successful individual from one who is less successful. Dress and grooming are significant factors in being hired for a job as well as being considered for advancement within the organization (Wisconsin Department of Workforce Development, n.d.).

6

©Image 100 Ltd.

Dressing for success in the interview typically requires a conservative business suit for both men and women.

6

DRESSING FOR SUCCESS

For some individuals, dressing for success is not a difficult task. These individuals have learned what clothing items best suit their body type and make the most effective presentation. For others, learning how to polish one's appearance is more challenging.

Have you ever had someone say, "You look particularly nice today"? Compliments such as this may be attributed to the design and color of clothing that is especially fitting to individual coloring and body type. Patterns, colors, and material of clothing can make a significant difference in your appearance. For example, knowing what colors complement your skin tone allows you to choose color combinations more wisely. By paying attention to your clothing and color selections, you can enhance your outward appearance and in turn feel more internally confident. Confidence contributes to overall success.

apply it

Dressing for Success Research

GOAL: *To develop further appreciation regarding what dressing for success means.*

STEP 1: Select at least one or two articles that are used as a reference for this chapter or find other articles that are of interest to you.

STEP 2: Read the article(s) and write a brief report on what you learned.

STEP 3: Consider placing this Dressing for Success Research report in your Learning Portfolio.

BODY TYPE

Dressing for success and selecting clothes that contribute to a positive impression and self-confidence involve understanding your body type. Certain clothing styles are more flattering to some body types than others. Careful selection of clothes can enhance the positive. The following are suggestions for clothes that work best for various body types (Pages, 2005):

> ▶ **The inverted triangle.** Individuals with this body shape are broader in the upper body than in the lower body. Clothing advice for these individuals includes:
>
>> ▶ Wear shirts with V-necks or open-neck shirts.

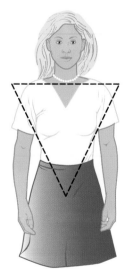

The inverted triangle body type is broader in the top half of the body.

- Avoid large patterns and bright colors on all clothing items and stick with one color (monochromatic outfits).
- For women, wear a long skirt that flares on the bottom to balance broadness in the upper body.
- Avoid tight shirts and shirts that have a lot of detail on the front.

- **The pear or diamond shape.** These individuals are essentially the opposite of the inverted triangle and are broader in the lower body than in the upper. These individuals may also have shoulders that slope. Clothing advice for this body shape includes:
    - Wear well-tailored pants and shirts with simple lines. Women should avoid gathered or full skirts. A skirt with a center seam can help to diminish wide hips. Longer skirts also can be more complimentary to a woman with heavy legs.
    - Wear long jackets with shoulder pads to balance the lower body.
    - Avoid wearing tight pants or skirts that are too tight.
    - Wear plain rather than decorative hosiery.
    - Wear colors that are not too dark.

- **The rectangle.** Individuals with a rectangle shape have evenly distributed weight between the upper and lower body. They may need to select clothing that gives the illusion of more shape. Clothing for individuals with this body shape includes:
    - Choose simple belts.
    - Layer garments.
    - For women, choose jackets, tunics, or vests over long skirts. Jackets should not end at the waist.
    - Select pants that are straight with stiff or pressed-down pleats.
    - Choose materials that retain their shape, such as crisp linens, cottons, twill, or tweed.
    - Materials with vertical patterns should be avoided.
    - Loose-fitting, oversized garments should be avoided.

- **Full figure.** Individuals with a full-figured shape or rounded figure will want to create the illusion of long, slim lines. Clothing selections should contribute to a shaped appearance. These can be accomplished as follows:
    - Avoid clothing that is too tight and hugs the body.
    - Avoid clothing that is too loose or too baggy, which can lead to a "dumpy" appearance.

The individual with a pear- or diamond-shaped body type is broader in the lower half of the body.

The rectangle body type is evenly proportioned between the upper and lower body.

6

▌ Select colors and textures that offer balance, as well as soft designs such as multicolored weaves.

▌ Wear skirts or pants with inverted pleats at the waist.

▌ Use belts that blend in with the outfit.

▌ Choose jackets that have straight lines and are defined at the waist.

Be aware that these body types are guidelines based on general categories, and most people find they are a combination of body types. Try various styles based on the type you think you are and use your best judgment to make your decisions. For any body type, the goal in selecting clothing is to look and feel your best. Let that be your guide.

apply it

Body Type and Skin Tone Appreciation

GOAL: **To help develop an understanding of how to dress for success, appreciating body type and skin tone.**

STEP 1: Form two groups of students. Have one group conduct research regarding body types and the other group research skin tones.

STEP 2: Look for information that can be presented to the class to provide insight into how to work effectively with the various body types and skin tones.

STEP 3: Give a presentation to the class using visual aids and activities that help individuals gain insight into their body type and skin tone.

STEP 4: Consider putting this Body Type and Skin Tone Appreciation report in your Learning Portfolio.

DRESSING FOR THE INTERVIEW

When deciding on appropriate dress for interviewing, the general consensus is that it is best to dress conservatively. A common standard is to dress one step up from the typical daily attire at the organization. It may be important to investigate the company where the interview will be taking place to confirm what attire will be appropriate. This can be accomplished by calling and asking someone in the human resource office or by visiting the company prior to the interview. Other considerations that affect dress choice are

The full figure or rounded body type is equally proportioned between the upper and lower body, but lines are less angular than the rectangle body type.

6

the type of job being applied for and the company dress expectations. For example, someone who is going to work as an airline mechanic will dress differently for the interview than someone who is applying for an executive position. If the airline mechanic applicant showed up in a three-piece suit, the employer might hesitate in hiring this individual, who is more than likely overdressed for the position. That is not meant to say that the airline mechanic should wear jeans to the interview. In fact, many employers find jeans to be unacceptable interview attire no matter what the job is. Much of the choice regarding what is worn to an interview depends on some common sense and having researched the corporate environment, culture, and the employer's preference.

So, what is acceptable? What if the company employees dress in office casual? Does their dress code affect how you dress for an interview or as a new employee? Does the interviewer's attire determine what you should be wearing? Here are some general thoughts from some professionals:

▶ No matter what your potential employer is wearing, the majority of employers will expect the interviewee to wear traditional interview attire (Larson, 2000).

▶ "The safest look for both men and women in an interview is traditional and conservative" (Brookhaven College Career Development Center, 2004, p. 1).

▶ "Even though the company may not require you wear a suit or professional wardrobe, you must put your best foot forward and wear it to the interview. Remember, it is a competitive market right now, and anything you can do to put yourself one step ahead of the competition is helpful" (Career Clinic, n.d.).

The most important thing to remember regarding the clothing you select for your interview is that your clothing must not get in the way of your presentation. You are there to sell your skills and abilities. You do not want your clothes to be the focus of the conversation!

GROOMING CONSIDERATIONS

Appropriate interviewing attire does include elements other than a good suit. A neat and clean appearance is perceived by many employers as being as important as the choice of dress. The following are grooming suggestions for before the interview:

▶ Hair style and care contribute to overall appearance. Hair should be clean and combed into an attractive style. If needed, get a haircut a week or two before the interview. For budget-conscious individuals, find a local beauty school that offers free or discounted haircuts.

6

▶ For men who choose to have facial hair, is important that facial hair be groomed and trimmed.

▶ Fresh breath during the interview is critical. Teeth should be brushed prior to the interview. Carry breath mints and use them before the interview as needed. Eating a small amount of food prior to the interview may also help maintain fresh breath by controlling unchecked stomach activity, but select mild foods that do not contribute to breath issues.

▶ Use deodorant. Avoid perfumes and scents.

▶ Appearance of fingernails can convey a professional image for both men and women. If money for manicures is a concern, see if a local beauty school in the area offers free or discounted manicures. If fingernail polish is worn, it should be clear or a soft, neutral color.

success steps

GROOMING FOR THE INTERVIEW

1. Keep hair neat and clean.

2. Select a hair style that complements your face shape and skin tone.

3. Make sure facial hair is groomed or removed.

4. Use deodorant and avoid perfumes and scents.

5. Make sure nails are manicured and appropriately colored if polish is used.

©Digital Vision

Well-selected interview attire for men includes a neutral color two-piece suit, solid color shirt in a neutral color, tie in complementary color, polished shoes, and minimal jewelry. Hair and nails should be well groomed. Cover tattoos and remove any body jewelry from piercings.

CLOTHING FOR THE INTERVIEW

Preparing for an interview and selecting clothing should be done as soon as the interview has been scheduled. Having at least two interviewing outfits is important. By keeping both outfits clean and ready, you will be prepared for any potential accidents that may occur. If the interviewing outfits have not been worn for a while, try each outfit prior to the interview day to make sure it fits properly. Dry clean or wash items as needed and complete any repairs such as missing buttons and frayed cuffs (Newberger, n.d.). Take care of other considerations prior to the interview, such as ensuring that shoes are polished and briefcase and/or purse is cleaned, polished, and well organized. If a winter coat will be needed, make sure that it is clean and ready to be worn.

Men's and women's clothing suggestions for interview attire are as follows (Brookhaven College Career Development Center, 2004; King's College Career Planning and Placement Office, n.d.):

Men:

▶ Suits are the most preferred outfit for interviewing. Common colors for suits are navy, brown, or shades of gray. Black is acceptable, but some may find it too dark or gloomy. Most professionals indicate that a two-piece suit is most appropriate.

▶ Shirts should always be long sleeved and be of solid colors: light blue, cream, or white. The fabric typically preferred is either a cotton-polyester blend or 100% cotton. Shirts must be clean and lightly starched.

▶ Tie colors should complement or blend with the overall outfit. The preferred fabric is 100% silk with a simple pattern. Once tied, the tie should have a small knot and extend down to the trouser belt. The acceptable width of ties is usually between 2¾ inches and 3½ inches. Bow ties should be avoided.

▶ Shoes should be well polished and in good condition, with no apparent scuff marks or other flaws. Black, brown, or burgundy leather shoes work best with business suits. Socks need to be dark, complement the suit, and be of calf length so that skin is not revealed when sitting down and crossing legs.

▶ Accessories such as belts should be selected to complement the shoes being worn. Jewelry should be minimal and typically include only items such as a wedding band, tie tack, watch, and cuff links. No earrings or other facial piercing rings should be worn to the interview. No accessories or clothing should have any words or images that indicate personal beliefs or political views. Tattoos should be covered when possible. Carry a leather briefcase that is in good condition. Make sure all of these items present a professional image.

6

success steps

MEN'S DRESSING TIPS

1. Select a neutral color, two-piece suit.

2. Select a long-sleeved shirt in a neutral color that complements the suit.

continued

Well-selected interview attire for women includes a neutral color, two-piece suit; a solid color blouse without added frills; polished, neutral color pumps; neutral color hose; and accessories that complement the shoes. Avoid plunging necklines and dramatic make-up. Do not carry both a briefcase and a purse; select one or the other. A briefcase is preferable. Cover tattoos and remove any body jewelry from piercings.

continued

3. Select a tie in a color that complements the shirt and suit.
4. Ensure that shoes are polished and scuff free.
5. Wear dark-colored, calf-length socks.
6. Keep jewelry to a minimum.

Women:

▶ Skirt suits are the recommended attire for women for an interview. Dresses are acceptable but are less appropriate than a suit. If a dress is worn, then a matching jacket is highly recommended. Casual slacks should never be worn unless research of the company has indicated otherwise. Color choices for suits are typically beige, charcoal, gray, black, or navy blue. Skirts of knee length or 2 inches above the knee are recommended, but skirt length may be selected according to body type.

▶ Blouses in solid colors that complement the skirt should be selected. White or cream is recommended. Styles chosen should be selected to complement one's body type. Avoid blouses with front frills or lace and plunging necklines.

▶ Generally, basic pumps with low or medium heels work best. Shoes need to be polished and in good condition. Colors that typically coordinate well with women's business suits include solid black, brown, navy, taupe, and burgundy. Panty hose must be new or in excellent condition and fit well to avoid any bagging at the ankles. Carry an extra pair just in case of an emergency. A neutral color that matches your skin tone is best.

▶ Accessories such as belts should be selected to complement or match the shoes being worn. Carry a briefcase rather than a purse. Carry a small, professional appearing purse if you do not have an acceptable briefcase. Do not carry both. Make sure the briefcase appearance and its contents, such as pen and paper, represent a professional image. Jewelry should be minimal and should only include items such as a wedding or engagement ring, necklace, earrings, bracelet, and watch. No more than one ring per hand should be worn. Earrings should not be dangly but close to the ear and should complement the entire outfit. No more than one set of earrings should be worn. Eyebrow or any other facial piercing jewelry should be removed. No piece of jewelry worn should draw too much attention.

▶ Make-up should be worn but needs to complement your skin tone rather than overwhelm your natural appearance. Dark eye shadows should be avoided. If nail polish is worn it should be a subtle tone, such as pale pink or a clear gloss.

success steps

WOMEN'S DRESSING TIPS

1. Select a neutral color, two-piece suit with a skirt of appropriate style for your body type.

2. Choose a suit over a dress. If a dress is worn, a jacket should be added.

3. Select a solid color blouse without added frills. Avoid plunging necklines.

4. Wear polished, neutral color pumps with a low to medium heel.

5. Wear neutral color hose.

6. Select accessories that complement the shoes.

7. A briefcase is preferred to a purse. Do not carry both a briefcase and a purse.

8. Select make-up that complements your skin tone and features but does not overwhelm.

▶ REFLECTION QUESTIONS

- What clothing do you own now that is appropriate for professional attire?
- What more can you learn about your skin tone and body type that might help enhance your appearance?

? CRITICAL THINKING QUESTION

6–2. What is your reaction to the following statement? "It isn't the clothes that make a person."

6

apply it

Interview a Professional

GOAL: To develop further appreciation of what is entailed in dressing for success.

STEP 1: Contact a professional in your field and arrange an interview. The purpose of the interview is to discuss the type of dress most appropriate for the profession.

STEP 2: For the interview, dress in clothing you believe is appropriate for interviewing with this individual. During the interview, ask the professional to critique your choice of dress and to offer suggestions for improvement.

STEP 3: Write a brief report on what you learned. Set goals for developing your professional wardrobe.

BUILDING A PROFESSIONAL WARDROBE ON A BUDGET

Often, college students find themselves without much additional cash. Consequently, budgeting for the eventual purchase of professional outfits needs to begin as soon as possible.

The Department of Apparel, Merchandising, Design and Textiles at Washington State University (n.d.) makes the following suggestions for dressing professionally on a tight budget:

▶ Don't wait until the last minute to start looking for the outfits you need to purchase. Since you are on a tight budget, finding the best clothes you can get for your money may take some time. Take your time and make wise purchases.

▶ Keep in mind that you are not just purchasing these outfits for the interview, but that these two outfits may need to serve you until you receive your first paycheck. Because of this, make sure the outfits can be mixed and matched to make a variety of outfits. Purchasing outfits with interchangeable components expands your possibilities and maximizes your wardrobe budget.

▶ Select a neutral tone such as black, dark gray, or navy around which to build your wardrobe. You can also choose contemporary colors such as pearl gray, steel blue, camel, and celery. When selecting colors, pay attention to those that best suit your skin tone.

▶ Do not overlook the important purchases of appropriate accessories and shoes. Budget these items into your overall plan.

▶ Purchase items that are washable to avoid dry cleaning expenses.

▶ If travel may be required for the interview and/or job, select clothing that is less likely to wrinkle.

▶ Although you are on a budget, do not cut corners when it comes to quality. Invest in clothing that is well made, of durable fabric, and of a classic design that is less likely to go out of style with the next clothing trend.

▶ Consider thrift shops when necessary. Often, thrift stores have merchandise that was worn minimally by executives and business people. Look for good name brands that offer quality. Inspect pieces for tears, frayed areas, and other signs of wear before purchasing. Check fabric for resistance to wrinkling by squeezing it in your hand.

▶ Finally, when in doubt, ask for help. Take someone shopping with you. This individual should be someone who has demonstrated the ability to dress professionally and whom you trust to help select the best items for your professional wardrobe.

success steps

PROFESSIONAL DRESSING ON A BUDGET

1. Begin budgeting early for your professional wardrobe.
2. Use the mix-and-match approach to stretch your wardrobe dollar.
3. Build your wardrobe around a neutral color base and add stylish, yet professional colors to your base.
4. Shop for quality rather than quantity.
5. Buy washable fabrics to minimize dry cleaning expenses.
6. Look for good-quality clothes in second-hand stores.
7. Seek the advice of an experienced and successful professional dresser.

REFLECTION QUESTION

- What concerns might you have about affording new outfits? What can you do to alleviate these concerns?

CRITICAL THINKING QUESTION

6–3. How can you learn to better appreciate the effects of dressing relative to your body type and skin tone?

CHAPTER SUMMARY

This chapter examined the elements of dressing for success in your job search. You considered the roles of elements such as body type and skin tone in the selection of clothing and how to select clothes based on these factors. Generally accepted standards of professional dress for interviews were also provided, as well as guidelines for accessorizing and attending to personal care issues. You also received suggestions for developing a professional wardrobe on a budget.

POINTS TO KEEP IN MIND

In this chapter, several main points were discussed in detail:

- Your dress and grooming is important and is a critical factor to getting hired.

- Accepting that your personal appearance does make a difference and working on doing what is necessary to make a good impression will be what differentiates a successful individual from a less successful one.

- By paying attention to clothing and color selections, individuals can enhance their outward appearance and in turn feel more confident.

▶ The presentation of your skills and abilities is the focus of the interview and is what needs to be heard. Don't let your clothes be the focus of the conversation.

▶ Being neat and clean is just as important as wearing the appropriate interview clothing,

▶ Establish a budget while still in college in order to be prepared to purchase the wardrobe items needed to dress for success.

LEARNING OBJECTIVES REVISITED

Review the learning objectives for this chapter and rate your level of achievement for each objective using the rating scale provided. For each objective on which you do not rate yourself as a 3, outline a plan of action that you will take to fully achieve the objective. Include a time frame for this plan.

1 = did not successfully achieve objective

2 = understand what is needed, but need more study or practice

3 = achieved learning objective thoroughly

	1	2	3
List appropriate clothing items that should be worn to an interview.	☐	☐	☐
Understand how first impressions can affect opinions of others.	☐	☐	☐
Explain how one's appearance can be improved by paying attention to dressing for one's body type and skin tone.	☐	☐	☐
Explain how one's outward appearance can affect one's internal confidence.	☐	☐	☐
Discuss considerations that should be given to one's interviewing attire.	☐	☐	☐
Discuss grooming tips that are important for professionals.	☐	☐	☐

Steps to Achieve Unmet Objectives

Steps   Due Date

1. _____   _____

2. _____   _____

3. _____   _____

4. _____   _____

SUGGESTED ITEMS FOR LEARNING PORTFOLIO

▶ Dressing for Success Research: This activity will develop your understanding of dress that is appropriate in your field.

▶ Body Type and Skin Tone Appreciation: Completing this activity will increase your awareness of your body type and skin tone and help you choose styles and colors that complement both.

▶ Interview a Professional: Interviewing a professional will increase your awareness of dress expectations in your field.

REFERENCES

Brookhaven College, Career Development Center. (2004). Dressing for the interview. Retrieved March 19, 2005, from http://www .brookhavencollege.edu/pdf/careerctr/interviewattire.pdf

Career Clinic. (n.d.). Dressing for the interview. Retrieved March 19, 2005, from http://www.careerclinic.com/pages/ dressingfortheinterview.asp

King's College, Career Planning and Placement Office. (n.d.). Tips on interviewing. Retrieved May 26, 2006, from http://www.kings.edu/ Academics/CareerPlanning/interv2.htm

Larson, B. (2000, Summer). Dressing for the interview at a business casual environment [Electronic version]. Republished from the New Jersey Staffing Alliance's *Staffing News.* Retrieved March 19, 2005, from the Top Echelon Web site: http://www.topechelon.com/jobseekers/ larson.htm

Pages, M. (2005). No body's perfect. Retrieved March 22, 2005, from http://www.geocities.com/bluegumtrees/image.html?200522

Newberger, N. (n.d.). Dress for success. Retrieved May 26, 2006, from http://www.worktree.com/tb/IN_dress.cfm

Washington State University, Department of Apparel, Merchandising, Design and Textiles. (n.d.). Dressing on a tight budget. Retrieved March 19, 2005, from http://amdt.wsu.edu/research/dti/Budget.html

Wisconsin Department of Workforce Development. (n.d.). Grooming for employment. Retrieved March 19, 2005, from http://danenet.wicip .org/jets/jet-4814-p.html

6

CHAPTER OUTLINE

Preparing for the Interview

Successful Interviewing Tactics

Interview Follow-Up

7 Successful Interviewing

THE BIG PICTURE

LEARNING OBJECTIVES

By the end of this chapter, you will achieve the following objectives:

▶ Explain the two types of questions that can be asked in a job interview.

▶ Discuss what makes an interview question illegal and explain appropriate responses to these types of questions.

▶ Understand accepted standards of interviewing.

▶ Discuss methods used to calm nerves before and during an interview.

▶ Define *nonverbal behavior* and provide examples of positive and negative nonverbal behavior in an interview.

▶ Discuss how to address your weaknesses or negatives in the interview.

▶ Discuss the purpose and methods of follow-up to an interview.

▶ Demonstrate the ability to find sample interview questions and create acceptable answers to each.

▶ Practice interviewing skills by participating in a mock interview.

TOPIC SCENARIO

As the company's Director of Human Resources, Julie spends much of her time interviewing applicants for various job openings. Julie's secretary just called her to tell her that the next applicant, Susan Edge, had arrived. Upon arriving in the lobby to meet Susan, Julie began her assessment of the applicant. Sitting in the lobby was a woman with a navy suit, pale pink blouse, and matching navy blue shoes. Beside her was an attractive leather briefcase. As Julie approached, the woman rose and introduced herself as Susan Edge. Julie noticed that Susan waited until Julie extended her hand in order to receive a handshake. After the introductions, Julie escorted Susan back to her office. Upon entering the office, Susan waited to be offered a chair and then both Julie and Susan sat for the interview. Prior to the first question, Susan asked Julie if it would be acceptable for her to take notes during the interview. The interview then began.

Based on this brief scenario answer the following questions:

▶ What did Susan do to help Julie begin to form opinions about her professionalism and abilities?

▶ How in this brief scenario did Susan demonstrate her abilities as a detail-oriented individual?

▶ What kind of impression did Susan make by waiting to accept Julie's handshake and waiting to be asked to sit?

▶ If Susan had extended her hand first or had sat before being offered a chair, what impressions, if any, might have been made? Should these actions affect Julie's overall opinion of Susan?

PREPARING FOR THE INTERVIEW

It is important to begin preparing for the interview as soon as it has been scheduled. Areas that require consideration when preparing for an interview include the following:

▶ Update your resume and reference list as needed and make copies to take to the interview.

▶ Prepare and organize your portfolio with anything that is related to the job. Refer to Chapter 3 for information on portfolio content and organization.

▶ Make sure what you will wear has been purchased and is clean and ready. Chapter 6 provided a detailed discussion regarding appropriate interview attire.

▶ Purchase any necessary pens, paper, or other materials that may be needed for the interview.

▸ Consult a map or map Web site to determine the best way to get to the interview location.

Another aspect of preparing for the interview includes conducting research on the company. Employers expect applicants for a position have taken the time to research the company and what the job entails. The Internet can usually provide useful information. Locate the company's Web site and familiarize yourself with the company's current projects, events, and issues. A company's annual report can also provide significant information. Other sources of information for research include the business section of the newspaper, trade associations and journals, directories found at local libraries such as Dun & Bradstreet's *Business Information Reports*, the manuals of Moody's Investor's Services, and Standard & Poor's guides, as well as company literature, newsletters, and business magazines (University of Dayton Career Services, n.d.(a)).

©Digital Vision

The Internet is an effective resource for conducting industry research related to your job search.

apply it

Researching Companies

GOAL: To develop more information regarding companies of interest.

STEP 1: Research three companies for which you might like to work.

STEP 2: From the information that you find, prepare a brief report of your findings. Are you still interested now that you know more about the company? Why or why not? What Web sites were used?

STEP 3: Share your information with the class.

STEP 4: Consider placing this company information in your Learning Portfolio.

In addition to conducting research, applicants need to fully understand what skills and abilities they are bringing to the employer. They also need to be able to specifically relate their skills to the requirements of the job. Employers want to know that the applicant they choose is the best fit for the required tasks of the job.

The best way to prepare for an interview is to

▸ Obtain and review the job description of the position for which you are applying. If possible, obtain a copy of the job description prior to the interview. If this is not possible, you may be able to obtain a description of a job that is similar enough to provide you information about the tasks and responsibilities that are desired for the job. See Figure 7–1 for an example of a job description.

7

Job Description

Position: Medical Assistant

Reports to: Physician/Nurses/Office Manager

Responsibilities:

The MA is responsible for the flow of patients through the office. Serves as a liaison between the patient and the physician and assists in ensuring quality patient care. Works directly with the physician and nurses in providing care to patients. Works with other ancillary departments such as radiology and lab in arranging testing and procedures for patients.

Duties include:

1. Obtains information regarding the patient's past history and current illness.
2. Takes and records vital signs of the patient including weight, temperature, pulse rate, respiration, and blood pressure.
3. Escorts patients to exam rooms and prepares patients for exams.
4. Assists physician with the treatment of the patient.
5. Assists the physicians in procuring lab samples and requisitions.
6. Schedules appointments for all referred cases.
7. Assists other office staff, when necessary, in making appointments, calling patients, locating charts, and filing reports in the medical chart.
8. Manages medical and drug supply inventory. Originates orders as needed.
9. Maintains sample supply closet.
10. Keeps examining rooms clean and stocked.
11. Properly disposes of contaminated and disposable items.
12. Assists in retrieving past medical records for patients as required for the patient's office visit.
13. Retrieves labs, x-rays, and other test results. Pulls appropriate patient chart and attaches report(s) to the file for physician viewing.
14. Conducts routine lab work and EKG's as ordered by the physician.
15. Performs other duties as assigned by the physician/office manager.

Job requirements:

Graduation from an accredited MA program and current certification.
Enjoy working with people in a positive productive environment.
Possess the verbal ability to understand patient medical records, physician orders and medication orders, to be communicative with the patient and hospital staff.
Possess the ability to deal tactfully and effectively with patients, parents, and other employees, hospital staff, and the physician.

FIGURE 7–1.   A job description outlines the responsibilities and expectations associated with a position. Doing an excellent job and advancing in your field often requires going above and beyond the expectations listed on the job description.

▶ Be clear on the knowledge that is necessary to do the job. Note the other skills and personal qualities that may be required or desired.

▶ If possible, discover what type of interview will be conducted. For instance, will it be a group interview, phone interview, online interview, or behavioral interview? Is the interview to take place over lunch or dinner?

▶ Anticipate the questions that may be asked and prepare answers in advance.

▶ Prepare questions that should be asked of the employer.

success steps

PREPARING FOR AN INTERVIEW

1. Review a job description, if possible. If a job description is not available, find out as much as you can about the position on the company's Web site or from Human Resources.

2. Be familiar with the knowledge you will need to do the job.

3. Find out what kind of interview will be conducted, if possible.

4. Anticipate questions that might be asked and how you would answer them.

5. Prepare questions to ask the employer.

INTERVIEWING QUESTIONS

An applicant will generally be asked two types of questions during an interview. Traditional questions seek factual information about an applicant, such as educational background and work experience. Situational questions ask the applicant to describe various situations and circumstances he or she has encountered. The purpose of situational questions is to assess more complex skills such as decision-making skills, use of ethical reasoning, and problem-solving strategies (University Career Services, n.d.). Being fully prepared for an interview requires the applicant to answer both the traditional and situational questions effectively and efficiently.

Depending on the company, more than one interviewer may attend the interview session. The purpose of a team interview is often to save both the employer's and the applicant's time. Although team interviews can be more challenging than the traditional one-on-one approach, it is important to mentally prepare for the possibility of a team interview. Caroselli (n.d.) suggests recognizing that team interviews are more stressful than traditional interviews and recommends making a connection with each interviewer and using

7

various examples from your experience rather than repeating the same example. Be prepared for the chance of a team interview, as you may not be informed in advance that a team approach will be taken. As with traditional interview formats, practicing, researching the company, preparing intelligent questions, and listening effectively contribute to a less stressful and more successful team interview. In addition, seek the assistance of your career placement personnel and conduct research to familiarize yourself with team interviewing.

Preparing for questions that may be asked during the interview takes time and thoughtful reflection. One way to anticipate questions that might be asked is to seek advice from an expert, such as career placement personnel at your school. Or, research commonly asked interview questions on the Internet, using "interview questions" as your search term. Once you have examples of questions, consider recording well-thought-out answers. Use the questions and answers to conduct the mock interview activity introduced later in this chapter with a friend, family member, or a professional in your chosen career. Have the "employer" ask questions to which you must appropriately respond. After the mock interview, ask the "employer" to evaluate how you conducted yourself and the answers that you provided. Be open to constructive criticism and repeat the mock interview as many times as necessary to improve in areas that are weak.

Common interviewing questions include the following (University of Dayton Career Services, n.d.(b)):

▶ Why should we hire you?

▶ What is your biggest strength/weakness?

▶ Why did you choose your major?

▶ Where do you see yourself in five years?

▶ What specific skills do you bring to this position?

The following list includes questions that may be more challenging to answer. Take time to write your answers down as you consider each question (Mulligan, n.d.):

1. What do you see yourself doing five years from now?

2. How do you make yourself indispensable to a company?

3. Tell me about a time when your course load was heavy. How did you complete all your work?

4. Tell me about a time when you had to accomplish a task with someone who was particularly difficult to get along with.

5. How do you accept direction and, at the same time, maintain a critical stance regarding your ideas and values?

6. What are some examples of activities and surroundings that motivate you?

7

REFLECTION QUESTION

- What types of questions do you think you might find most challenging in an interview? What steps do you need to take to become more comfortable with these questions?

7. Tell me how you handled an ethical dilemma.

8. Tell me about a time when you had to resolve a problem with no rules or guidelines in place.

apply it

Writing Interview Questions and Answers

GOAL: *To demonstrate the ability to write interview questions and provide appropriate answers.*

STEP 1: Write at least 30 questions that you think may be asked in an interview. For each question, provide a response.

STEP 2: Ask your instructor to review the questions and answers and make suggestions for improvements.

STEP 3: Consider the career placement personnel at your school as an additional resource for this exercise.

STEP 4: Consider putting your questions and answers in your Learning Portfolio.

There are some questions that employers cannot legally ask due to the nature of the questions. It is important for applicants to be aware of what these questions are and how to respond professionally to any such question that might be asked. Questions asked during an interview must pertain to the position and your ability to effectively perform tasks associated with it. The following are areas about which employers are prohibited from asking questions (University Career Services, n.d.; University of Dayton, n.d.(c)):

▶ birthplace, nationality, ancestry or descent of applicant, applicant's spouse, or parents

▶ marital or family status

▶ gender, race, color

▶ religion or religious days observed

▶ membership in organizations associated with a particular race, religion, or ethic group

▶ information about arrests, disabilities, or health conditions unrelated to job performance. Employers *are* permitted to ask questions about an applicant's ability to perform a specific task that is related to the job. For example, an employer can ask you if you can lift 30 pounds if that is a requirement of the job. The employer is prohibited from asking you if you have any disabilities.

7

If an illegal question is asked, it is probably unintentional. As a job applicant, it is important to respond professionally to any question that appears to be illegal. If handled correctly, the interviewer will not be made to feel uncomfortable as the question is left unanswered. Here are a few options for responding to illegal questions as recommended by the University Career Services of George Mason University (n.d., "Responding to Challenging Questions").

Option 1. Explore the meaning behind the question or its intent and respond to that meaning.

▌ For example, your response to "where were you born?" might be, *"If you are wondering about my status, I am authorized to work in the United States."*

▌ Your response to a question about marital status or young children might be, *"If you are concerned about my ability to travel, let me assure you that I am prepared to make all the necessary arrangements so that I can travel the amount of time you indicated is likely in this job."*

Option 2. Ask about the relationship of the information to the job.

▌ For example, if asked about your place of birth: *"I'm not sure what my place of birth has to do with my qualifications for this position."* Wait for a response from the interviewer and see if he or she can explain how this question connects to the job requirements. You can at this point choose to either answer the question or decline.

Option 3. Tactfully remind the interviewer that if not related to the job, such questions are illegal or inappropriate. However, with this approach you run the risk of coming across as uncooperative or confrontational. Avoid taking this tactic if at all possible. Keep in mind that illegal questions posed by the employer are typically not asked with any malicious intent (University of Dayton, n.d.(c)).

Option 4. Answer the question to avoid confronting the interviewer and possibly hurting your chances of being hired.

? CRITICAL THINKING QUESTION

7–1. What is your reaction to the following statement? "If an employer asks me a question that I do not want to answer, I will just tell the interviewer I am unable to answer the question."

7

SUCCESSFUL INTERVIEWING TACTICS

Preparing for the interview will significantly help in the overall success of the experience. In addition to considering questions and your answers, what you will wear, and the materials you need for the interview, a few other simple rules should be followed for a successful interviewing experience. The following suggestions for a successful interview can help reduce stress and increase confidence (Hansen, n.d.):

▶ Make sure you know how to get to the interview. If necessary, do a dry run a day or two before the interview to make sure you know how long it will take to get there. Arriving at least 10 to 15 minutes ahead of the scheduled interview is suggested; arriving late to an interview is unacceptable. If a late arrival is unavoidable due to an emergency, call the company to alert the employer to the situation. Remember that a late arrival for any reason will make a poor impression. Always call as far in advance as possible if you must cancel the appointment. Do not simply fail to show up for the interview. If this occurs you not only ruin your chances for getting the job, but your actions show disrespect for the employer's time, as the time could have been used for interviewing someone else. Remember, too, that the professional world is a small one and word does travel. Your actions toward one employer may influence your chances with another.

▶ On the day of the interview, allow extra time for preparing and driving to the interview site. Allow for traffic and other possible delays.

▶ The night before the interview, prepare your briefcase with all the necessary items, such as copies of your resume, reference list, and portfolio. Take two or three pens and some paper. Consider all necessary items/information you may be required to supply the employer. For example, having the names and addresses of references might be beneficial should the interviewer request them.

▶ Take your cell phone for any last-minute calls you might need to make or to use in the event of an emergency. However, be sure to turn it off when you arrive at the interview.

▶ If you are not going directly to the interview from home, Pillsbury (n.d.) suggests that an "emergency kit" may be useful. Include items such as "an umbrella, an extra tie/pair of stockings, breath mints, a comb, an extra pair of glasses or contacts, tissues or a handkerchief, and few safety pins."

▶ As you arrive for your interview, present a calm and organized demeanor. If you have prepared effectively and allowed ample time, you will avoid arriving breathless and harried. Arrive with a pleasant friendly smile, greet the receptionist with professionalism, and offer your first and last name. Establish good eye contact as you speak. Remember that first impressions can make a difference.

▶ If a job application is presented to you, fill it out neatly and provide correct and accurate details as required.

7

EFFECTIVE PARTICIPATION IN AN INTERVIEW

1. Familiarize yourself with the location of the interview before the actual date.

2. On the day of the interview, allow extra time for preparing and arriving at the site.

3. Prepare your briefcase with necessary items ahead of time.

4. Take your cell phone. Be sure to turn it off when you arrive.

5. If you are not going to the interview from home, take an emergency kit of items that you can use to freshen up if necessary before the interview.

6. Enter the interview setting with a calm and organized demeanor.

7. Complete any paperwork that is requested.

DEALING WITH FEELINGS OF NERVOUSNESS

Most individuals feel nervous at interviews. The following are a few suggestions to help you calm feelings of apprehension, based on Bowman (n.d.).

▶ **Have realistic expectations.** Avoid elevating the position to your "dream job" or, conversely, telling yourself that you will never land the job. Keep the job prospect in perspective and focus on preparing for and doing your best in the interview.

▶ **Know what you bring to the job.** Establish a clear relationship between your experience and skills and the requirements of the job. Be able to articulate this relationship clearly and directly.

▶ **Prepare.** Research the company, update your resume and portfolio, and ready your wardrobe, all of which has been emphasized in this chapter. Thorough preparation and a working knowledge of your resume, the company, and the position can increase your confidence and reduce anxiety.

▶ **Take care of yourself.** Pay attention to your physical well-being. Get ample rest the night before your interview, eat a healthy and well-balanced meal beforehand, and avoid foods that don't agree with you.

▶ **Familiarize yourself with the interview site.** In addition to ensuring that you will be on time for the interview, arriving early provides you with an opportunity to focus and center your energy. Getting a brief overview of your surroundings can reduce nervousness. A stop in the restroom to ensure that you look your best will also help you relax.

success steps

DEALING WITH FEELINGS OF NERVOUSNESS

1. Have realistic expectations.
2. Know what you bring to the job.
3. Prepare.
4. Take care of yourself.
5. Familiarize yourself with the interview site.

Some individuals perspire more when anxious. If this is the case for you, make sure you have put on fresh deodorant and powder. Wear clothing that allows your body to breathe. If the interview room is warm, ask if it is acceptable to take off your jacket. It is better to be comfortable than dripping wet during the interview. Prior to shaking the interviewer's hands, wash your hands with hot water. This will eliminate or minimize sweaty and clammy palms.

The Santa Clara University Career Center (n.d., p. 1) suggests asking yourself the following questions to alleviate some of your anxieties by addressing fears objectively:

◗ What do I fear most about the interview situation?

◗ What is the worst thing that can happen?

◗ If I were giving advice to someone else in this situation, what would I tell him/her?

Nonverbal behaviors, such as eye contact and shaking hands, communicate as much about you as (perhaps more than) what you say.

7

THE IMPORTANCE OF NONVERBAL BEHAVIORS

An applicant's nonverbal behavior is just as important as the responses he or she gives to the interviewer's questions. During the interview, applicants need to be aware of what they might be communicating through their nonverbal behaviors. Nonverbal behaviors include your facial expressions, posture, and hand gestures. Examining and adjusting body language and appearance is critical to interview success and making a positive impression on the employer. The following examples illustrate how positive body language can make a difference (University of Dayton Career Services, n.d.(d)):

◗ Smile as you enter the office. A sincere smile indicates an approachable individual. Avoid a forced smile, but do appear friendly and pleasant.

◗ Convey confidence. Approach the interviewer and office staff with a self-assured manner. An erect posture and direct eye contact communicate assurance and poise.

The purpose of the interview is to provide both the applicant and potential employer the opportunity to exchange information and determine whether the position and applicant are a good fit.

7

▶ Offer a firm handshake. A firm handshake also communicates confidence and sincerity. Ensure that your handshake is neither too weak nor too strong and that the length of the handshake is appropriate. A weak handshake can indicate a lack of assertiveness, low self-confidence, and a lack of investment in the interview. Conversely, a handshake that is too strong can convey aggressiveness. A handshake that lasts too long can indicate nervousness and a lack of ability to modulate emotions such as excitement (University of Dayton Career Center, n.d.(e)).

▶ Carry your briefcase and coat in your left hand so that your right is free during introductions to shake hands.

▶ Make it a point to remember the interviewer's name and its correct pronunciation.

▶ Use a posture that conveys interest and attentiveness. Straight posture and leaning forward slightly with appropriate eye contact is recommended.

▶ Rest your hands in your lap or on the arms of the chair. If you are sitting at a table, you may rest your arms on the table with your hands folded loosely. It is acceptable to use hand gestures to emphasize your points, although not excessively. Folding your arms across the body is not recommended, as it may communicate nervousness or defensiveness.

▶ Pay attention to your mannerisms. Be aware of and avoid mannerisms that might be perceived as negative and annoying, such as playing with your hair.

success steps

NONVERBAL COMMUNICATION DURING THE INTERVIEW

1. Smile. Do not force a smile, but do appear approachable and friendly.
2. Convey confidence with your erect posture and direct eye contact.
3. Use a firm handshake.
4. Carry your briefcase in your left hand so that your right is free to shake hands.
5. Make it a point to remember the interviewer's name.
6. Demonstrate attentiveness by sitting straight and leaning forward slightly toward the interviewer.

7. Rest your hands in your lap, on the arms of the chair, or folded loosely on the table in front of you.

8. Use hand gestures in moderation.

9. Pay attention to your mannerisms and avoid those that are distracting or annoying.

HANDLING THE INTERVIEW

The purpose of an interview is not necessarily to get a job. Most of the time the purpose of the interview is to provide more information to the applicant and employer to determine if the fit is right. Often, an applicant really does not know if the job is right for him or her until the interview has taken place. Sometimes during the interview, either one or both of the parties may conclude that the job is not a good fit. This does not mean that the interview was a failure. The interview is only a failure if the applicant neither presented him- or herself professionally nor expressed his or her skills and abilities clearly enough for the employer to choose the right candidate for the job.

Once the interview begins, it is important to remain calm and confident. The preparation that has been done prior to the interview supports a relaxed and effective presentation. The following are some suggestions to help make the interviewing experience more positive (Bellevue University Career Services, n.d.; Hansen, n.d.):

▶ Not all individuals are perfect at the job of interviewing. If your interviewer is less than effective, it is your job as the applicant to remain courteous and answer the questions as asked. Provide thorough and effective information. Having difficulty with an individual interviewer does not necessarily mean you will not get the job. Remain professional and do not run the risk of ruining your chances due to an interviewer's inadequacies.

▶ Turn off all cell phones and pagers prior to entering the interview.

▶ Do not allow family members, children, friends, or other individuals to accompany you to an interview.

▶ Request a cup of water prior to the beginning of the interview. Nerves often create dry mouth. Do not chew gum or suck on a breath mint during the interview. Avoid yawning as it can indicate boredom.

▶ Answer each question with consideration and care. Some questions may not seem as important as others, but the interviewer probably has good reason for asking each one.

7

▶ Prior to answering a question, it is acceptable to pause and make sure your answer is well thought out. Moments of silence are reasonable in order to prepare a thoughtful response. Demonstrating the ability to reflect on and think through an answer reflects the ability to consider relevant issues and attend to details.

▶ Avoid making jokes and being overly friendly with the interviewer. You want to appear professional.

▶ Use good grammar. Avoid pausing words such as *um* or *uh*. Taking a moment to reflect and plan what to say is preferable.

▶ Speak up. Soft-spoken individuals may be seen as lacking confidence.

▶ Demonstrate effective listening skills. Never interrupt the interviewer. Effective listening will communicate a desirable workplace skill and enable you to answer the question more appropriately.

▶ Clarify questions as needed. It is appropriate to ask questions if you do not understand something. Clarifying questions will allow you to provide more effective and appropriate answers.

▶ Be positive about your experiences and achievements, but avoid exaggerating or embellishing the truth. Doing so will catch up with you later.

▶ When responding to questions, be as clear and succinct as possible. Whenever possible, answer questions with more than just a "yes" or "no." Provide examples when possible to further explain answers, but avoid rambling.

▶ Avoid topics such as religion and politics. If the interviewer brings up any controversial topics, remain vague and noncommittal. It is inappropriate to share your opinion.

▶ When answering questions, do not hesitate to demonstrate the knowledge you have gained about the company through your research. Employers will appreciate your efforts. Avoid being cocky about your knowledge, which may be perceived as showing off.

▶ Avoid discussion of your personal life.

▶ Avoid criticizing a former employer or colleague. If you experienced difficulties or are asked about a difficult time, describe the situation as a positive learning experience. Accept responsibility that is yours and describe how you would change for the better.

▶ Avoid overuse of hand gestures. If this is a natural inclination, then try folding your hands together on your lap. This will also help those who have a tendency to chew their nails (Dress for Success, n.d.).

▶ If you trip or accidentally knock something over, do not panic. Showing you can handle these types of incidents demonstrates that you handle pressure well (Dress for Success, n.d.).

▌ Always have some questions written down that you want to ask the employer. By asking questions you demonstrate your interest and intelligence.

▌ Focus on what you offer the company and how your abilities meet company needs. "Always keep the focus on what you can do for the company; the interviewer is most concerned with your ability to do the job and benefit the company, not with the company's ability to meet your expectations" (Bellevue University Career Services, n.d., "Selling Yourself during the Interview").

▌ Avoid appearing desperate for the job. The employer may begin to wonder why you have not been hired anywhere.

▌ Do not bring up salary and benefits. Salary negotiation will be covered in detail in Chapter 8. Bellevue University Career Services (n.d.) makes the following suggestions regarding salary and benefit discussions:

  ▌ Salary is typically discussed in later interviews. Wait for the employer to raise the issue of salary and benefits. After the issue is mentioned, it is appropriate to ask questions.

  ▌ Wait until the interviewer offers a salary figure before stating your expectations. If you are asked to identify an amount, ask what the salary range is for the position. If you have a minimum acceptable salary figure, it is acceptable to state it, but realize that doing so may eliminate you from consideration if the amount is not acceptable to the employer.

  ▌ Keep in mind that benefits also contribute to the total package. Benefit packages that include health and life insurance, retirement plans, and other features are costly and can add significant value to your salary.

▌ If you are interested in the job at the end of the interview, tell the interviewer. Ask about the next step in the hiring process, to demonstrate interest. Find out when you should expect to hear from the employer.

▌ Obtain the name and title of the interviewer at the end of the interview. Get a business card if possible. It is appropriate to send the interviewer a thank-you note as follow-up to the interview.

▌ After you have left the company, spend a few minutes in your car or at a quiet place taking notes on your experience. Jot down your thoughts and further questions that may need researching.

It is difficult to totally fail in an interview. Employers typically are understanding about the stress that applicants are experiencing, and many employers do their best to alleviate applicants' anxieties.

success steps

INTERVIEWING SUCCESSFULLY

1. Remain courteous under all circumstances and answer the questions as asked.

2. Turn off all cell phones and pagers prior to the interview.

3. Do not allow family members, children, or friends to attend the interview.

4. Request a cup of water prior to the beginning of the interview in the event your mouth becomes dry.

5. Answer each question with consideration and care.

6. Prior to answering a question, it is acceptable to pause.

7. Avoid making jokes and being overly friendly with the interviewer.

8. Use good grammar. Avoid pausing words such as *um* or *uh*.

9. Speak up to avoid being seen as lacking confidence.

10. Demonstrate effective listening skills. Never interrupt the interviewer.

11. Clarify questions as needed.

12. Be positive about your experiences and achievements, but avoid exaggerating.

13. When responding to questions, be as clear and succinct as possible.

14. Avoid topics such as religion and politics.

15. When answering questions, do not hesitate to demonstrate the knowledge you have gained about the company through research.

16. Avoid discussion of your personal life.

17. Avoid criticizing a former employer or colleague.

18. Avoid overuse of hand gestures.

19. If you trip or accidentally knock something over, handle the situation with grace and poise.

20. Always have some questions written down to ask the employer.

21. Focus on what you offer the company and how your abilities meet company needs.

22. Avoid appearing desperate for the job.

23. Do not bring up salary and benefits.

7

24. If you are interested in the job at the end of the interview, tell the interviewer.

25. Obtain the name and title of the interviewer at the end of the interview so that you can send a thank-you note.

26. After you have left the company, spend a few minutes in your car or at a quiet place to record notes about your experience.

Addressing Your Weaknesses

Addressing your weaknesses can be one of the most challenging aspects of the interview. Knowing that honesty is essential, many struggle with how to present weaknesses in the most positive light. University Career Services (n.d.) lists the following common shortcomings that become apparent during an interview and suggests the following guidelines for addressing them.

▶ **Lack of related experience.** Draw on experience other than work such as that gained in school, through hobbies, or in volunteer experience. Consider skills that you have that are similar and can be applied to the experience you lack.

▶ **Lack of education or degree.** Emphasize skills you have developed through on-the-job training or other experiences, as well as self-taught knowledge and skills.

▶ **Poor academic performance.** Present examples of learning activities in which you have performed well. Point out other accomplishments and emphasize how they relate to the position you are seeking.

▶ **Frequent job changes.** Emphasize what you learned from your various jobs, especially as it might pertain to the job for which you are interviewing. Show how your job changes illustrate a pattern of professional growth. Explain how this job fits with your interests and goals.

▶ **Gap in employment.** Describe what you did during the gap in your employment history and what you did and learned during this period of time. If you were fired or quit a job, share what you learned from the experience.

Poor performance in an interview can be attributed to a variety of reasons. In addition to failing to address perceived negatives, other reasons for presenting poorly in interviews include doing too much talking and not enough listening, being arrogant, not communicating well, devaluing or overvaluing one's abilities and worth, and failing to clarify the responsibilities of the job

▶ REFLECTION QUESTION

• What scares you or makes you nervous about interviewing? How can you overcome these fears?

? CRITICAL THINKING QUESTIONS

7–2. If you lack experience in the job you are applying for, how can you address this weakness in a positive light?

7–3. How can you address other weaknesses, such as a poor academic record, frequent job changes, or others?

by asking appropriate questions (Weinstein, 2001). By practicing interviewing skills and gaining confidence in your abilities, you will become more successful in the interviewing process.

apply it

Mock Interviews

GOAL: To demonstrate the ability to perform in a mock interview.

STEP 1: Select a partner with whom you will complete this activity,

STEP 2: For the first round, one of you will act as the employer and the other as the job applicant. Using the questions developed in the Writing Interview Questions and Answers activity, ask and answer questions. Understand the importance of treating this exercise with as much sincerity and seriousness as you would an employment interview. After one of you has played the role of the employer and the other the applicant, switch roles and repeat the exercise.

STEP 3: After the exercise, reconvene as a class and discuss what was learned in the mock interviews, what areas were difficult, and how you might continue to improve.

INTERVIEW FOLLOW-UP

Following up after the interview is essential and can be done in a variety of ways. The first important step is to write a thank-you letter to the interviewer(s). If the interview was a team effort, send individual notes to each member. Thank-you letters can be handwritten only if your handwriting is neat. If not, type the letter and personally sign it. Ensure that the spelling of names and titles is correct. Send your thank-you note(s) as soon as the interview is over. The employer will appreciate your quick response. E-mails are acceptable but should still be followed with a traditional written thank-you note. This will make the thank-you more personal. Figure 7–2 provides an example of a thank-you letter.

At the end of the interview it is important to ask the employer when further contact from the company should be expected. If you have not received word within the designated time frame, it is acceptable to contact the employer to ask about the status of the hiring process (Santa Clara University Career Center, n.d.). If it is necessary to leave a message, provide your

REFLECTION QUESTIONS

- How well do you think you will do in your interviews?
- What are your plans to minimize the concerns that you still have about interviewing?

7

William Running Deer
432 East Brooks Avenue
Denver, CO 80000

November 20, 2005

Ms. Christina Chung
Human Resources Director
Everett Technologies
10067 Mountain View Road
Broomfield, CO 82222

Dear Ms. Chung:

Thank you for taking the time yesterday to meet with me regarding the office manager position at Everett Technologies. The programs we discussed seem to be leading the company in exciting new directions. I believe that my experience with and knowledge of streamlining systems and tracking data would greatly facilitate your implementation of these new programs. In addition, the positive relationships I have developed with office staff in the past have provided me with a foundation for working effectively with diverse individuals in the office setting.

Everett Technologies' innovative and forward thinking perspective is impressive and I believe I could contribute significantly to your growth. I would appreciate your serious consideration of my candidacy for the office manager position.

Thank you again for the opportunity to meet with you and learn about your company. I look forward to hearing from you.

Sincerely,

William Running Deer

FIGURE 7–2.   An effective thank-you letter acknowledges the employer's time spent and the information provided as well as highlights your skills and positive perceptions of the position and organization.

correct phone number(s) and the best time to reach you. If you have not received a return call within 24 hours, follow up with another call. Unfortunately, some employers are not considerate in following up with job applicants. If you have had no return calls after leaving two or three messages in a week's time, then it may be necessary to assume that the job has been filled. It may be helpful to contact an individual other than the interviewer at the company, such as the director of human resources, to determine the status of the position. Make sure throughout the process that your efforts do not become bothersome to individuals at the company. Maintain a positive professional demeanor at all times.

? CRITICAL THINKING QUESTION

7–4. What is your reaction to the following statement? "It feels awkward to do mock interviews. They don't feel real and I just don't think the practice makes a difference."

CHAPTER SUMMARY

This chapter provided you with the foundation for preparing for and participating effectively in a job interview. Suggestions for preparing included updating your resume and reference list, organizing your portfolio, and preparing responses to potential interview questions. You reviewed strategies for successful interviewing as well as methods for minimizing nervousness before and during the interview. The impact of nonverbal behaviors on the interview was emphasized. You learned ways to address your weaker areas during the interview and reviewed general behaviors that are likely to contribute to a less stressful and more successful interview. Finally, you learned appropriate interview follow-up techniques, such as sending thank-you notes to the interviewer(s) and appropriately maintaining contact with the employer to track the outcome of the interview.

POINTS TO KEEP IN MIND

In this chapter, several main points were discussed in detail:

- Conducting research about the company where one will be interviewing is an important step to successful interviewing.
- Job applicants must be able to clearly and succinctly explain their strengths and abilities during the interview.
- Interviewing questions can be divided into two main categories: traditional and situational questions. To fully be prepared for an interview, an applicant must be able to answer both types of questions effectively and efficiently.
- Conducting mock interviews as practice can substantially increase success in employment interviews.
- It is illegal to ask certain types of questions during an interview. The job applicant must be familiar with what constitutes illegal questions and how to professionally respond if such questions are asked.
- An applicant's nonverbal behavior is just as important as the responses given to the interviewer's questions.
- An interview is only a failure if the applicant fails to present himself or herself professionally and fails to express his or her skills and abilities clearly enough for the employer to choose the right candidate for the job.
- Various types of interviews can occur, including one-on-one interviews, phone interviews, online interviews, and group

interviews. Applicants need to be prepared for any interview type they encounter.

▌ Follow-up after the interview is essential and can be done in a variety of ways, including sending an e-mail, writing a letter, and calling. Calls and e-mails should *always* be followed with written correspondence.

LEARNING OBJECTIVES REVISITED

Review the learning objectives for this chapter and rate your level of achievement for each objective using the rating scale provided. For each objective on which you do not rate yourself as a 3, outline a plan of action that you will take to fully achieve the objective. Include a time frame for this plan.

1 = did not successfully achieve objective

2 = understand what is needed, but need more study or practice

3 = achieved learning objective thoroughly

	1	2	3
Explain the two types of questions that can be asked in a job interview.	☐	☐	☐
Discuss what makes an interview question illegal and explain appropriate responses to these types of questions.	☐	☐	☐
Understand accepted standards of interviewing.	☐	☐	☐
Discuss methods used to calm nerves before and during an interview.	☐	☐	☐
Define *nonverbal behavior* and provide examples of positive and negative nonverbal behavior in an interview.	☐	☐	☐
Discuss the purpose and methods of follow-up to an interview. Discuss how to address your weaknesses or negatives in the interview.	☐	☐	☐
Demonstrate the ability to find sample interview questions and create acceptable answers to each.	☐	☐	☐
Practice interviewing skills by participating in a mock interview.	☐	☐	☐

Steps to Achieve Unmet Objectives

Steps   Due Date

1. _____   _____

2. _____   _____

3. _____   _____

4. _____   _____

SUGGESTED ITEMS FOR LEARNING PORTFOLIO

▌ Researching Companies: This activity will increase your awareness of important issues at companies of interest and contribute to effective interviews skills.

▌ Writing Interview Questions and Answers: Writing interview questions and answers will prepare you to answer actual interview questions more effectively.

▌ Mock Interviews: Practicing interviewing skills in mock interviews will give you practice for an authentic interview.

REFERENCES

Bellevue University Career Services. (n.d.). Strategies for effective interviewing. Retrieved March 19, 2005, from http://career.bellevue.edu/~career/intervue.htm#TOP

Bowman, C. B. (n.d.). Keeping a lid on interview anxiety. Retrieved November 6, 2005, from the Dow Jones Career Journal Web site: http://www.careerjournal.com/jobhunting/interviewing/19980812-bowman.html

Caroselli, M. (n.d.). How to survive a team interview. Retrieved November 5, 2005, from the Dow Jones Career Journal Web site: http://www.careerjournal.com/jobhunting/interviewing/19990630-caroselli.html

Dress for Success. (n.d.). Interview tips: Do's and don'ts. Retrieved March 19, 2005, from http://www.dressforsuccess.org/interview_tips/dosanddonts.asp

Hansen, R. S. (n.d.). Job interviewing do's and don'ts. Quintessential Careers. Retrieved March 19, 2005, from http://www.quintcareers.com/interviewing-dos-donts.html

Mulligan, B. (n.d.). Interviewers' favorite questions . . . and answers. Retrieved March 28, 2005, from http://www.jobweb.com/Resources/Library/Interviews/Interviewers_92_01.htm

Pillsbury, Ceil. (n.d.). Dress for success. University of Wisconsin-Milwaukee. Retrieved March 19, 2005 from the Career and Life Help Page: http://www.uwm.edu/~ceil/career/jobs/index.html

Santa Clara University Career Center. (n.d.). Interviewing & dressing for success. Retrieved March 19, 2005, from http://www.scu.edu/careercenter/resources/publications/interviewing.pdf

University Career Services. (n.d.). Interview questions . George Mason
    University. Retrieved March 28, 2005, from http://careers.gmu.edu/
    students/jobhunt/huntref/questions.htm

University of Dayton Career Services. (n.d.(a)). How and why to research
    a company. Retrieved March 19, 2005, from http://careers.udayton
    .edu/articles/articles.asp?research.txt

University of Dayton Career Services. (n.d.(b)). How to prepare for an
    interview. Retrieved March 19, 2005, from http://careers.udayton
    .edu/articles/articles.asp?intviewtips.txt

University of Dayton Career Services (n.d.(c)). Questions employers
    should NOT ask during an interview. Retrieved March 19, 2005,
    from http://careers.udayton.edu/articles/articles.asp?cannotask.txt

University of Dayton Career Services. (n.d.(d)). First impressions DO
    count!. Retrieved March 19, 2005, from http://careers.udayton.edu/
    articles/articles.asp?firstimpress.txt

University of Dayton Career Services. (n.d.(e)). The importance of a good
    handshake. Retrieved March 19, 2005, from http://careers.udayton
    .edu/articles/articles.asp?handshake.txt

Weinstein, B. (2001). Five biggest interview blunders. ITworld.com.
    Retrieved March 19, 2005, from http://www.itworld.com/
    Career/1834/ITW010426interview2/

7

CHAPTER OUTLINE

Purpose of Negotiation

Assessing and Negotiating a Job Offer

Do's and Don'ts in Negotiating

Accepting or Declining a Job Offer

8 Negotiation

THE BIG PICTURE

CHAPTER	
10	100%
9	90%
8	**80%**
7	70%
6	60%
5	50%
4	40%
3	30%
2	20%
1	10%

LEARNING OBJECTIVES

By the end of this chapter, you will achieve the following objectives:

▶ List areas that should be evaluated when assessing a job offer.

▶ List some of the more common benefits offered by employers.

▶ Explain the purpose of negotiating.

▶ Discuss how personal, professional, and family goals can influence job negotiations.

▶ Describe the process involved in assessing a job offer.

▶ Understand the benefits typically covered in an employment relocation package.

▶ Explain the steps involved in successful negotiating.

▶ Demonstrate how to effectively negotiate a salary.

▶ Demonstrate the ability to write a letter for declining a job offer.

TOPIC SCENARIO

Joe Ward, a recent graduate of his local community college, has been searching for a job. During his job search, he has had numerous interviews with a variety of companies. There are two companies from which Joe would particularly like to receive an offer. If he gets offers from both, Joe is unsure about how he will decide which job to take, since both jobs offer different but excellent opportunities.

Today, Joe received offers for both of the jobs he wanted. One job offers slightly more money than the other but lacks some benefits that the other job offer provides. Joe is faced with a difficult decision.

Based on this short description of Joe's dilemma, answer the following questions:

- What should Joe consider when he is trying to make a decision regarding which job offer to accept?

- What resources might Joe use to help him make this difficult decision?

- What issues do you think are most important for Joe to consider?

- In what areas might Joe consider negotiating with the offering companies? If Joe decides to negotiate, what approach should he take with the companies?

- Have you ever been in this position? If so, what did you do? Was your choice the best decision? If not, what have you learned from your own experience?

PURPOSE OF NEGOTIATION

Receiving job offers can be both exciting and daunting due to the variety of decisions that must be made. These decisions include whether the offer should be accepted as is or if further negotiations are necessary. Negotiation can result in an offer more closely matched to your wishes, which will increase your overall satisfaction with the final package. Ultimately, a job applicant wants to be sure that he or she makes the right decision in accepting or declining a position.

The most important issue that applicants need to consider is the effect that accepting or declining a job offer will have on their own personal goals, professional goals, and family goals (Hoover, 2006). It is important to evaluate each of these areas in order to determine if negotiations are needed to better satisfy these important goals. For example, the job that you accept can affect your earning potential, which influences your family's goals. Likewise, the setting in which you work will offer you specific opportunities for your professional growth. Being aware of these considerations and needs is essential to effective long-term planning. If you have done effective research (see Chapters 1 and 7) into the companies you are considering, you will have a clear idea of what each offers.

ASSESSING AND NEGOTIATING A JOB OFFER

Understanding when negotiations are appropriate requires skill in assessing numerous aspects of the job offer and knowing what areas can be negotiated. Areas to be considered include the organization and its culture, nature of the job, future opportunities, and salaries and benefits (U.S. Department of Labor Bureau of Labor Statistics, 2004).

ASSESSING THE ORGANIZATION

Before beginning the application and interviewing process with an organization, an applicant has typically conducted some research to gain knowledge about the organization. Further questions can then be asked of the employer during the interviewing process. Information helpful to research includes areas such as the financial condition of the company, its size, years in existence, and reputation. Knowing these aspects of a company will help you to decide whether the company is a match for your personal and professional goals. This type of information can be accessed using a variety of methods, including conducting research at the local library or on the Internet, where materials such as annual reports, press releases, company newsletters, and trade magazines may be accessed (U.S. Department of Labor Bureau of Labor Statistics, 2004). Other directories that may be helpful to reference include the following sources, which you may have accessed for preliminary company research:

- *Dun & Bradstreet's Million Dollar Directory*
- *Standard and Poor's Register of Corporations*
- *Mergent's Industrial Review* (formerly *Moody's Industrial Manual*)
- *Thomas Register of American Manufacturers*
- *Ward's Business Directory*

> ### REFLECTION QUESTIONS
>
> - What personal, professional, and family goals do you have that could be affected by the type of job you accept?
> - What concerns or fears might you have when it comes to negotiating a job offer?

> ### CRITICAL THINKING QUESTION
>
> 8–1. What is your response to the following statement? "Negotiating skills are overrated. It is totally up to the employer what the job offer will be."

©Digital Vision

Use the Internet to research a company prior to your interview to learn about the organization's achievements, size of the company, and its corporate culture. Knowing as much as possible about an organization will allow you to ask effective questions as well as appear knowledgeable and invested in the position.

8

The U.S. Department of Labor Bureau of Labor Statistics (2004) suggests keeping the following questions in mind when evaluating an organization:

1. Does the organization's business or activity match your own interests and beliefs? For example, if you are a health care worker but believe abortion is wrong, then working at a facility that performs abortions would not be advised. You will be more dedicated to an organization that conducts business that matches your interests and beliefs.

2. Will the size of the organization affect the type of opportunities available to you for advancement? "Large firms generally offer a greater variety of programs and career paths, more managerial levels for advancement, and better employee benefits than do small firms. Large employers also may have more advanced technologies. However, many jobs in large firms tend to be highly specialized" (U.S. Department of Labor Bureau of Labor Statistics, 2004, "How will the size of the organization affect you?").

3. Are you willing to work for a company that is new or does the stability of a well-established organization appeal to you? Some individuals are willing to take the risk with a newer company due to the possibility of sharing in the company's future successes. Others may determine that the possibility of job loss is too high a risk.

4. Does the company have a good reputation within the community? Your future professional opportunities could be affected negatively or positively depending on the reputation of the company you are working for.

UNDERSTANDING THE JOB

Prior to accepting an offer, it is important for the job applicant to have a clear picture regarding the nature of the job. Areas to consider include (U.S. Department of Labor Bureau of Labor Statistics, 2004):

- job location
- duties, responsibilities, and hours of the job
- turnover rate of the job. If turnover rate is high, what are the reasons?
- future opportunities available within the organization and how these opportunities can be acquired by accepting the current job offer
- salary and benefits including pay raises, travel allowance, and continuing education

NEGOTIABLE FACTORS

When an offer is made, it is important to determine what areas can be negotiated. The following factors can often be negotiated (Hoover, 2006):

- ▶ location of the position
- ▶ relocation benefits
- ▶ start date
- ▶ when appraisal reviews will be conducted and salary increases received
- ▶ sign-on bonus
- ▶ salary
- ▶ overall benefits package

Job Location and Relocation Benefits

Advancements in technology and computers have significantly increased flexibility in job location. Many jobs can be performed either at home or at a satellite office. If relocation is required, it is important to research the community in which you would be living to ensure that the location is desirable. If a job applicant must relocate, the company may offer a benefits package to help defray relocation costs. Receiving this benefit does sometimes depend on the level of the position. Many organizations do not offer candidates at an entry-level position a relocation benefits package. If a relocation package is offered, the following benefits may be included (Quintessential Careers, n.d.(a)):

- ▶ house-hunting trip expenses
- ▶ lodging fees
- ▶ moving expenses
- ▶ mortgage/closing fees
- ▶ brokerage fees
- ▶ temporary housing expenses
- ▶ spouse re-employment expenses

Start Date

Even though the employer may have a specific start date for beginning work, this does not mean that negotiating a different start date is impossible. Negotiating a start date is important depending on the applicant's situation. It is better to inform the employer of any issues that require a postponement of the start date than to accept the start date with full knowledge of conflicts that may create problems later.

8

Schedules of Appraisal Reviews and Salary Increases

Some employers give bonuses for job performance. Salary increases are often attached to appraisal reviews. "If the organization incorporates this type of appraisal system it might be possible to ask for an earlier review to increase your earnings sooner than normal" (Hoover, 2006, "Factors That May Be Negotiated").

Sign-On Bonuses

Sign-on bonuses may be an option, depending on the industry you are entering. A sign-on bonus is "an agreed upon amount of money given to you at the time of your acceptance of the offer" (Hoover, 2006, "Factors That May Be Negotiated"). If the employer's need for your expertise is high, it may be possible to negotiate a larger sign-on bonus.

Salary

Prior to applying for any position, job applicants need to determine the potential salary range for each job and how that compares to their budget requirements. Applying for a job that offers a salary significantly lower than your budget requirements is not wise. If the expected salary is close to the required amount, then it may be realistic to negotiate the desired salary. Job applicants should always establish a minimum salary requirement. It is also important to understand the difference between hiring range and salary range. Hiring range is the range within which a starting salary is determined, based on the expertise of the new hire. Salary range is the range of the salary for the position over the course of employment. The top of the salary range indicates the highest amount you can earn in that position unless the range is increased. Hiring range is where you will start on the pay scale. Salary range has more long-lasting implications, as it tells you the maximum amount you can expect to earn over time in the position. Knowing your personal and professional goals will help you to determine whether the salary range is appropriate for you.

Your minimum salary requirement is based on your financial needs. By setting a realistic budget, job applicants can more clearly differentiate needs from desires. Finding a high-paying entry-level job may not be realistic. Establishing what is realistic will assist you in making wise choices.

Another determining factor affecting salary is the reality of what can be earned for the type of position and industry you are entering. It is reasonable to want to earn as high a salary as possible, but it is irrational and frustrating to expect an unrealistic amount. It is wise to research a realistic salary so that your expectations are realistic. Consider the following resources for researching salaries:

- ▶ Salary.com
- ▶ JobStar: Profession-Specific Salary Surveys

- SalaryExpert.com
- Bureau of Labor Statistics
- Securities and Exchange Commission
- The American Almanac of Jobs and Salaries
- Professional trade journals and business magazines
- Newspaper and online job listings

Establishing the acceptable range allows for the job applicant to more accurately access what the employer is willing to do. If hiring and salary ranges are below your expectations, begin the negotiation process, which will be discussed in the subsequent sections of this chapter.

Typically, a salary offer is not made until all interviews have been completed. An offer can be written or verbal. If an offer comes in person or by phone, you need not accept the offer at that very moment. It is always good to ask for some time to consider all the details of the job offer, including the salary. The following are some other tips for negotiating salary (Hansen, n.d; CollegeGrad.com, 2006):

- **Know the reasonable limits.** Complete effective industry research to determine the realistic salary range in your field. Know what is fair considering your geographic region, education, and demand for employees in your industry. You don't want to undersell yourself, nor do you want to price yourself out of the running.

- **Aim high.** When negotiating a salary, it is wise to request (within reason) a higher salary than what you are willing to accept. The employer is likely to make a lower counterproposal to your offer, so by proposing a higher amount, you are more likely to complete your negotiations closer to your goal. A key factor in the success of this approach is to keep your request within reasonable limits.

- **Negotiate to your strength.** If you are a skilled speaker, ask to discuss a counter proposal in a meeting. If you communicate better in writing, then send a counterproposal letter. Examples of counterproposal letters can be found on the Internet. Conduct a search using "salary counter proposal letters" as your search terms.

- **Avoid (as much as possible) naming a specific salary.** During the interviewing process, the employer may ask you what your salary expectations are. When this occurs, it is wise not to mention a specific amount to avoid losing out by stating too low a salary or, conversely, missing out on the job because you have asked for an unrealistic sum. If you have completed effective industry research, you will know what is fair. If you are asked about your salary requirements, it is wise to respond by asking what the hiring range is for new graduates in the position. Respond by indicating whether the range is acceptable or not. You can tactfully indicate that the range is competitive with or below that offered by other organizations.

▶ **Remember other benefits in the package.** If the salary is not negotiable, consider negotiating other benefits. For example, you may request a signing bonus, higher performance bonuses, or a performance review and raise to be completed sooner than is typical. Examples of nonmonetary benefits to consider include time off, a flexible work schedule, or other benefits such as insurance packages.

▶ **Negotiate with a win-win attitude.** Realize that you need to exhibit flexibility when possible. Hansen (n.d.) suggests, "Never make demands. Instead, raise questions and make requests during negotiations. Keep the tone conversational, not confrontational." Negotiations must be done professionally and thoughtfully if you really want the job.

---

success steps

PREPARING FOR NEGOTIATING

1. Know the reasonable limits.

2. Negotiate to your strength. For example, if you communicate most effectively in writing, negotiate in writing.

3. Aim high.

4. Remember other benefits in the package. These can also be negotiated.

5. Negotiate with a win-win attitude.

---

apply it

Salary Research

GOAL: *To develop an awareness of a realistic salary expectation in a specific field.*

STEP 1: Conduct research on the Internet and/or at the library regarding the salary ranges you are likely to find in your field.

STEP 2: Write a brief report summarizing your findings.

STEP 3: Consider placing the salary research in your Learning Portfolio.

8

Overall Benefits Package

Although salary is a critical aspect of a job, the benefits package can often compensate for a less desirable salary. It is important for job applicants to understand and appreciate that benefits can add up to 30% of the total compensation package (Quintessential Careers, n.d.(b)). The following are some of the more common benefits offered by employers:

- medical insurance
- dental insurance
- optical/eye care insurance
- life insurance
- accidental death insurance
- business travel insurance
- disability insurance
- vacation days
- paid holidays
- sick/personal days/family leave
- 401(k) plan
- pension plan
- profit sharing
- stock options/Employee Stock Ownership Plan (ESOP)
- tuition reimbursement
- health club membership
- parking, commuting, and business expense reimbursement

Developing your negotiating skills as well as gaining as much knowledge as possible about a company will support your efforts to achieve your employment goals.

DO'S AND DON'TS IN NEGOTIATING

8

Since the ultimate goal of negotiating is to get what you want, developing effective negotiating skills is critical to success. Kelly (2000) presents the following steps to successful negotiating:

- **Step 1: Prepare.** Knowing a company's hiring practices and goals will inform you of the company's priorities and define the value of the skills that you bring to the organization's long-term plans. Use the research you have completed to prepare you with this critical knowledge.
- **Step 2: Know what you can about the hiring dynamics.** If you are a highly desirable candidate because of your expertise or because

you are one of a few or the only applicant, your strategies will be different than if you were one of several qualified applicants. Knowing the dynamics of the hiring situation will define the amount of bargaining leverage that you have.

▶ **Step 3: Be professional.** The individuals with whom you are negotiating are your potential coworkers. Negotiate in a manner that demonstrates your professionalism.

▶ **Step 4: Know your needs and limits.** Entering the negotiation process with a clear understanding of your own needs will allow you to negotiate reasonably. A clear picture of what you need and want as well as issues on which you can yield will allow you to more easily see if and when negotiations have succeeded or failed.

▶ **Step 5: Respect the employer's position.** As you have limits regarding what you can and cannot accept, so does the employer. Be aware and respectful of budget constraints and other limitations, such as fairness to current employees of the employer. You are not expected to accept something that cannot meet your needs, but it is important to recognize when the employer cannot go beyond certain limitations.

▶ **Step 6: Use your judgment.** Remember that what you say during the negotiation process is up to you. Of course, be honest, but approach problems and concerns in a manner that helps your position. Total candor is not always necessary and may not be appropriate in all situations. By divulging too much, you may be offered less than what the company was willing to offer you originally.

▶ **Step 7: Remember that there's more than salary.** Remember that you have other points of negotiation in addition to salary. If it fits your needs, you can also negotiate for an earlier performance review and raise, request additional time off in lieu of pay, or bargain for other available benefits.

▶ **Step 8: Stay focused on your goal.** Your goal in the negotiation process is to achieve an employment package that meets your needs. The negotiation process is not one of winning or losing, but one of reaching a mutually agreeable employment situation. Don't focus on winning, and never make the employer feel as if he or she were a loser.

▶ **Step 9: Remain objective.** Part of professionalism is remaining objective and rational. State your position clearly and without signs of emotion. Emotional outbursts diminish your professionalism and are likely to work against you in the negotiation process.

▶ **Step 10: Know when to stop.** Know when you have achieved your goal or when it is clear that the employer is unable to meet your requests. Likewise, do not push for more than you reasonably need. Avoid appearing greedy and unreasonable, which may cause the employer to reconsider the offer that has been made.

▶ **Step 11: Get it in writing.** As with any business transaction, it is important to get a written agreement summarizing the offer. If possible, have an attorney review the written agreement to ensure that all elements are appropriately documented prior to accepting the offer.

success steps

NEGOTIATING SALARY SUCCESSFULLY

1. Prepare.
2. Know what you can about the hiring dynamics.
3. Be professional.
4. Know your needs and limits.
5. Respect the employer's position.
6. Use your judgment.
7. Remember that there's more than salary.
8. Remain goal directed.
9. Remain objective.
10. Know when to stop.
11. Get it in writing.

apply it

Negotiating a Salary

GOAL: To demonstrate the ability to effectively negotiate a salary.

STEP 1: Divide students in the class into pairs.

STEP 2: Using scenarios provided by the instructor, role-play negotiating a salary with an employer. One student will be the employer and the other student the job applicant. Treat the role-playing seriously, since this activity can help prepare you for real-life salary negotiation situations. After the role-playing is completed, the "employer" should constructively critique the job applicant on his or her negotiation abilities.

continued

REFLECTION QUESTIONS

- What areas of negotiation do you know you need to work on?
- How do you plan on improving your negotiation skills?

? CRITICAL THINKING QUESTION

8–2. What is your response to the following statement? "Men are better at negotiating than women."

Effective negotiation can lead to an employment agreement that is acceptable to both employer and applicant. In addition, it is wise to obtain a copy of the agreement in writing.

8

continued

> Where could the job applicant improve? What did the applicant do right? If needed, redo the role-playing to provide practice in negotiation skills. Reverse roles to allow for each student to represent the employer and the job applicant.
>
> **STEP 3:** Write a brief report on what you learned from this activity and consider putting this information in your Learning Portfolio.

ACCEPTING OR DECLINING A JOB OFFER

When accepting a job offer, it is important to make sure that what is agreed upon is documented in writing. This documentation typically comes from the company in the form of a letter of offer or letter of agreement. If this is not a common practice of the employer, ask the employer to provide you a letter of agreement that briefly outlines what has been discussed. Inform the employer that you need to have some sort of documentation of agreement for your own personal records. This should not be an issue and later may protect you if any disagreements occur. Make sure to obtain this documentation prior to your start date.

If you verbally decline an offer, it is still important to write a professional letter declining the offer (Machowski, n.d.). Always respond to an employer's offer. Not responding is unprofessional and takes up valuable time that the employer will need to find another applicant.

When preparing the letter of decline, keep in mind the following four steps suggested by Machowski (n.d.):

Step 1. Call the employer to decline the offer and then send a formal letter to decline the offer. Send the letter immediately after the employer has been verbally informed.

Step 2. Prepare the letter as you would any other professional correspondence. Respond professionally and courteously so that you maintain a professional relationship with the organization. The contacts at this company may be worth having in the future.

Step 3. In the letter there is no need to discuss in detail your future plans or why you are declining. It is acceptable to say that you have decided on a different position that more closely matches your career objectives. Be gracious and express your appreciation for the offer. State your positive impression of the company and let the company know that you seriously considered the offer.

Step 4. Be clear and concise. Say what needs to be said and then end the letter professionally.

▶ REFLECTION QUESTION

- What has your experience been so far regarding accepting or declining an offer from an employer? Did you at any time feel as if you could have handled the situation more professionally? If so, how will you improve your methods next time?

❓ CRITICAL THINKING QUESTION

8–3. What message are you sending by not responding to an employer's offer?

8

Sample letters for declining a job offer can be found on the Internet. Conduct a search using "letters for declining a job" as your search term.

apply it

Letter to Decline a Job Offer

GOAL: To demonstrate the ability to write a letter declining a job offer.

STEP 1: Conduct research on the Internet and/or library to find examples of letters for declining job offers.

STEP 2: Create your own letter utilizing the examples as a guide. The letter should be representative of what you would send to an employer. First drafts should be given to the instructor for review. Write a final draft incorporating the instructor's feedback and representing what would be sent to the employer.

STEP 3: Consider placing the examples and your Letter to Decline a Job Offer in your Learning Portfolio.

CHAPTER SUMMARY

This chapter focused on the elements of job negotiation. You learned the many areas to consider, including personal, professional, and family goals. In addition to these areas, aspects of the job, such as the nature of the job, growth potential, and salary and benefits, must be considered. You learned strategies for negotiation as well as methods for accepting and declining offers.

POINTS TO KEEP IN MIND

In this chapter, several main points were discussed in detail:

- When considering a job offer, the most important issue that applicants need to consider is the effect that the decision to accept or decline will have on their personal, professional, and family goals.

- Assessing a job offer entails evaluating areas such as the organization, the nature of the job, future opportunities, salary, and benefits.

- Areas that are typically negotiable include location of the position, relocation benefits, starting date, when appraisal reviews will be conducted, when salary increases will be received, sign-on bonus, salary, and overall benefits package.

▶ Prior to accepting any job offer, job applicants should ask for some time to consider all the details.

▶ Negotiating successfully requires being prepared.

▶ A good negotiator seeks a win-win situation for everyone.

▶ Prior to accepting a job offer, always get a written statement of employment terms.

▶ Declining a job offer should be done both verbally and in writing.

LEARNING OBJECTIVES REVISITED

Review the learning objectives for this chapter and rate your level of achievement for each objective using the rating scale provided. For each objective on which you do not rate yourself as a 3, outline a plan of action that you will take to fully achieve the objective. Include a time frame for this plan.

1 = did not successfully achieve objective

2 = understand what is needed, but need more study or practice

3 = achieved learning objective thoroughly

	1	2	3
List areas that should be evaluated when assessing a job offer.	☐	☐	☐
List some of the more common benefits offered by employers.	☐	☐	☐
Explain the purpose of negotiating.	☐	☐	☐
Discuss how personal, professional, and family goals can influence job negotiations.	☐	☐	☐
Describe the process involved in assessing a job offer.	☐	☐	☐
Understand the benefits typically covered in an employment relocation package.	☐	☐	☐
Explain the steps involved in successful negotiating.	☐	☐	☐
Demonstrate how to effectively negotiate a salary.	☐	☐	☐
Demonstrate the ability to write a letter for declining a job offer.	☐	☐	☐

Steps to Achieve Unmet Objectives

Steps   Due Date

1. _____   _____

2. _____   _____

3. _____   _____

4. _____   _____

SUGGESTED ITEMS FOR LEARNING PORTFOLIO

▶ Salary Research: This activity will give you an understanding of realistic salary ranges in your field.

▶ Negotiating a Salary: This activity is intended to provide you with practice in developing your negotiation skills.

▶ Letter to Decline a Job Offer: This activity is intended to provide you with practice declining a job. Feedback that you receive will allow you to develop your skills.

REFERENCES

CollegeGrad.com (2006). The money response technique. Retrieved June 9, 2006, from http://www.collegegrad.com/jobsearch/ 16-29.shtml

Hansen, R.S. (n.d.). Job offer too low? Use these key salary negotiation techniques to write a counter proposal letter. Quintessential Careers. Retrieved March 30, 2005, from http://www.quintcareers.com/ salary_counter_proposal.html

Hoover, Myrna. (2006). Negotiating job offers guide. The Career Center, Florida State University. Retrieved June 1, 2006, from http://www .career.fsu.edu/ccis/guides/negotiate.html

Kelly, S. (2000). The do's and don'ts of negotiation. Network World. Retrieved March 30, 2005, from the ITworld.com Site Network Web site: http://www.itworld.com/Career/1727/ITW2109/

Machowski, D. A. (n.d.). Declining a job offer. Mount Holyoke College Career Development Center. Retrieved March 30, 2005, from http:// www.mtholyoke.edu/offices/careers/recruit/toolkit/decline.htm

Quintessential Careers. (n.d.(a)). Salary negotiation and job offer tutorial: Relocation expenses. Retrieved March 30, 2005, from http://www .quintcareers.com/salary_relocation.html

Quintessential Careers (n.d.(b)). Salary negotiation and job offer tutorial: Be sure to evaluate the entire compensation package. Retrieved March 30, 2005, from http://www.quintcareers.com/salary_package.html

U.S. Department of Labor, Bureau of Labor Statistics. (2004). Evaluating a job offer [Electronic version]. Occupational Outlook Handbook. Retrieved March 30, 2005, from http://www.bls.gov/oco/ oco20046.htm

8

CHAPTER OUTLINE

The Importance of Etiquette in the Job Search

Job Search Etiquette

Etiquette in Special Situations

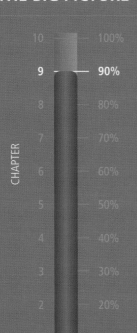

9

Professional Courtesies in the Job Search

THE BIG PICTURE

CHAPTER

10 — 100%
9 — 90%
8 — 80%
7 — 70%
6 — 60%
5 — 50%
4 — 40%
3 — 30%
2 — 20%
1 — 10%

LEARNING OBJECTIVES

By the end of this chapter, you will achieve the following objectives:

▶ Explain the importance of utilizing proper etiquette during the job search.

▶ Discuss ways that job applicants can demonstrate good manners.

▶ Describe the considerations that a job applicant should make when using a cell phone for an interview.

▶ Discuss the standards of effective phone interviewing.

▶ Explain important considerations to make when an interview is conducted over a meal.

▶ Demonstrate the ability to use good phone manners during a phone interview.

Etiquette and courtesy demonstrated during the job search reveals much about how you treat other people and how effectively you work with others.

TOPIC SCENARIO

Nearing the end of her college education, Joan has sent out letters of application to a number of employers. Today, Joan received a call from an employer who had received her information and wants to conduct an initial interview by phone. The interview is scheduled for tomorrow at 2:00 p.m.

Based on this scenario, answer the following questions:

▶ How should Joan prepare for the phone interview?

▶ Would Joan prepare differently for the phone interview as opposed to an in-person interview? If so, how?

▶ What considerations should Joan make to ensure that the interview runs smoothly?

▶ What phone courtesies should Joan demonstrate?

▶ If Joan is using a cell phone, what are the additional considerations? What should she do differently?

THE IMPORTANCE OF ETIQUETTE IN THE JOB SEARCH

Something as simple as etiquette—good manners—can seem like an insignificant thing. However, the social appropriateness that you demonstrate in the job search speaks to your professionalism and how you will manage your conduct on the job. An employer appreciates being treated courteously, and doing so makes a favorable impression. In addition, consider the messages that etiquette sends.

▶ **How you will represent the organization.** The consideration and courtesy that you demonstrate during the job search process provides the employer with an example of how you will treat customers or clients. The way in which clients are treated forms the public image of the company and either attracts business or discourages it. Employers want to hire individuals who will represent their company in a positive manner.

▶ **Messages about you as a person.** The consideration that you show others contributes to the reputation you are building as a professional. Professional circles are frequently small, and word travels. Even if you are not hired by a particular employer, your reputation is being established based on your interactions and your manners.

9

apply it

The Importance of Proper Etiquette

GOAL: *To gain an understanding of the importance that employers place on applicants utilizing proper etiquette.*

STEP 1: Schedule an interview with a professional in your chosen field. The purpose of the interview is to inquire as to the importance that the employer places on proper etiquette and how proper etiquette should be exhibited by job applicants.

STEP 2: Write a short report regarding your findings and be prepared to share it with the class.

STEP 3: Consider placing the report regarding the Importance of Proper Etiquette in your Learning Portfolio.

JOB SEARCH ETIQUETTE

Professionalism can be demonstrated in various ways, including the use of proper etiquette. There are many opportunities for job applicants to demonstrate proper etiquette throughout the application process. It is important to remember that employers not only seek a technically qualified individual, but also look for an individual who has the capability to follow general principles of good manners and professionalism. The following are some general guidelines that a job applicant can utilize to demonstrate good manners (Caroselli, 2000):

▶ **Respond immediately to any communication received from an employer.** Follow up the employer's call, letter, or e-mail and inform the employer if you are accepting or declining his or her invitation. Do not be rude by neglecting to follow through. Even if you are not interested in continuing with the company, you need to inform the employer of this decision. It is important to do so graciously and maintain a positive professional relationship throughout the process of withdrawing an application or declining an offer.

▶ **Never be late.** If an employer tells you to call at a certain time, then make sure you call on time. Show up for the interview on time or even a little early. Being on time demonstrates respect for the other person's time.

▶ **Demonstrate politeness.** Politeness can be demonstrated by saying words such as *please, thank you,* and *excuse me.* Say "thank you" and "please" to the receptionist and other individuals with whom you have contact. Remember the importance of establishing good first impressions.

▶ **Pay attention to time.** Be aware of rambling. Employers are busy individuals who want applicants to answer questions clearly and concisely. During your conversations and interviews with the employer, be mindful of his or her time. Glancing discreetly at one's watch is appropriate. Quickly come to a stopping point if you see time is running out. The employer will greatly appreciate your attention to this matter. If the employer chooses to extend the time, that is his or her choice. The job applicant should be willing to stay as long as the employer requires.

▶ **Listen well.** Employers want to share information about the company and the job with applicants. Although some of the information may be public knowledge, show an interest. Never yawn or stare off into space, as doing so demonstrates poor manners.

▶ **Be aware of your body language.** Sit up and demonstrate attentiveness. Straight yet relaxed posture with a slightly forward lean, direct eye contact, and an occasional nod communicate enthusiasm and interest. In addition to interest, direct eye contact indicates honesty. Avoid crossing your arms, as doing so can be interpreted as anger or a closed attitude. Positive body language communicates much about your attitude and how you are approaching the employment opportunity.

▶ **Demonstrate passion and interest in the company and the job.** Actions such as making follow-up calls to learn the status of the interviewing and decision-making processes demonstrate your investment. Take the initiative to bring to the interview items such as a portfolio of your work to demonstrate your abilities and dedication to your work. The more you demonstrate passion for the company and the job, the more the employer will see you as a potential candidate.

▶ **For any interview, be prepared.** A lack of preparedness can indicate a lack of interest. If an employer asks if you have any questions, make sure you do! Those who fail to ask questions can be viewed as uninterested.

▶ **Perform a job-related task if asked.** Some employers will have applicants perform a job-related task to see if the applicant is qualified for the job. Graciously perform the task to the best of your ability and never refuse to perform the task requested by the employer. Refusal indicates lack of confidence and lack of ability.

9

▶ **Send a postinterview thank-you note.** A survey conducted by the staffing firm Accountemps found that "more than 76% of employers like receiving a post-interview thank-you note, but only 36% of applicants write them" (Caroselli, 2000). Thank-you notes should be sent immediately after the interview. The content of the thank-you note should include thanking the interviewer for his or her time, offering to provide additional material as needed, and stating an interest in working for the company.

▶ Never renege on an agreement you make with a company. When you have accepted a position with an organization, you must stop interviewing with other companies. The employer is depending on you and has possibly lost the chance to hire their second choice, due to the time that has passed. In addition, word travels in the professional world and you may be hurting your reputation.

success steps

PROPER ETIQUETTE IN THE JOB SEARCH

1. Respond immediately to any communication received from an employer.

2. Be on time for any interview or appointment with an employer.

3. Demonstrate politeness by demonstrating courtesies such as saying "please," "thank you," and "excuse me," and waiting to be offered a seat.

4. Pay attention to time and be aware of rambling. Speak succinctly and to the point.

5. Listen well. Pay attention to information about the organization and show interest in what the employer tells you.

6. Be aware of your body language.

7. Demonstrate passion and interest in the company and the job.

8. For any interview, be prepared. Use the research you have completed on the company and have questions ready to demonstrate your interest.

9. Some employers will have applicants perform a job-related task to see if the applicant is qualified for the job. Graciously perform the task.

10. Send a postinterview thank-you note.

11. Never renege on an agreement you make with a company.

REFLECTION QUESTIONS

- Do you typically demonstrate good manners?
- With what areas of etiquette could you become more familiar?

? CRITICAL THINKING QUESTION

9–1. How do you respond to the following statement? "As an employer I would never hire an individual who demonstrates poor manners."

©Image Source Limited

Although telephone interviews can be more casual in some respects (such as attire), they should be treated as a professional appointment by minimizing distractions and having relevant documents in front of you. Pay particular attention to your verbal communication, as the interviewer does not have the benefit of responding to non-verbal behaviors.

9

ETIQUETTE IN SPECIAL SITUATIONS

General etiquette considerations are important in all professional interactions and activities. There are situations that may arise during the job search process that require attention to specific details that are unique to the situation. Traditional interviewing was covered in Chapter 7. The following less traditional interviewing methods are included here because of their unique demands and the special etiquette considerations they require.

PHONE INTERVIEW ETIQUETTE

Demonstrating phone etiquette is an important element of the job search process. Initial contact with a company often occurs by phone. Employers call the contact numbers job applicants provide on their resumes. The importance of this information being accurate is critical to job search success. Voice mailboxes and answering machines are frequently used to receive messages. Job applicants must ensure that these devices are set up with an appropriate message that demonstrates both professionalism and proper manners. Entertaining messages that may be amusing to your friends are not always appropriate when you are expecting return calls from prospective employers. Change any whimsical messages to something straightforward and professional. Proper messages include examples such as (Crawford Hentz, n.d.(a), "Pre-contact"):

> ◗ "You've reached Brenda, Cathy, and Mark. Please leave a message."
> ◗ "You've reached the Sizemores. Please leave a message."
> ◗ "You've reached 617-973-5235. Please leave a message."

If you rely on other people to take messages for you, it is your responsibility to ensure that these individuals also understand and use proper phone etiquette and take messages accurately.

When you receive a message from an employer, phone etiquette requires you to return the message in a timely manner. When returning the call, it is important to give your full first and last name, along with the reason for your call. Always be polite and repeat information as required. Be aware of rate of voice and pitch. Speak clearly and distinctly.

If you receive a call from an employer directly, don't defer the employer. It is best to put aside what you are doing and take the call promptly. However, there may be circumstances when you are preoccupied with another task or rushing to get to an appointment and are truly unable to give your undivided attention. In this case, it may be best not to take the call and return the call when you are able to focus. If you answer the phone, good phrases to use in this situation would be "'I'm so happy you called. I have about 10 minutes before I have to run out the door. Is that enough time, or can I call you back later this afternoon?' This way, you are expressing your interest, being clear about the time you have, and suggesting a time to connect later" (Crawford Hentz, n.d.(a), "When you're there for the contact").

CELL PHONE INTERVIEWS

With the increased use of cell phones versus land lines, job applicants do need to make sure that cordless phones and cell phones are fully charged when possible. If the battery is low, inform the employer at the beginning of the call and ask if you can call him or her back immediately using a different phone. If you use a cell phone as your primary phone, inform the employer at the time of the call and indicate that a call back will be immediate if a disconnect occurs. Make sure to get correct callback numbers. If hearing the employer is difficult due to a poor cell phone signal, check that you understand each other. Crawford Hentz (n.d.(a), "When you're there for the contact") suggests saying, "I'm having trouble hearing you. Can you hear me clearly?" It is less acceptable to ask the employer to speak up, which can sound abrupt and demanding. At the end of the call, make sure to thank the employer for his or her time and follow up the phone call with a thank-you letter.

Phone interviews should be treated with as much care and attention as you would give to an in-person interview. Although getting hired solely from the phone interview is unlikely, it does offer the opportunity for the employer to get to know you and to draw conclusions about whether further conversations should occur.

For further information regarding successful phone interviewing, consider the following recommendations from Crawford Hentz (n.d.(b)):

▶ Ensure that the contact information in your cover letter and resume is correct.

▶ Make sure your answering machine or voice mail message is professional.

▶ Keep by the phone a list of companies to which you have sent your resume. That way, you will not be caught off guard when an employer calls.

▶ Be prepared for a telephone interview just as you would for an inperson interview. Do your research just as you would for a traditional interview.

▶ Find a location where you will not be disrupted during the phone interview.

▶ Take notes of your conversation as you would during an in-person interview. Make sure note taking does not get in the way of good listening skills.

▶ Indicate if you are not able to hear the employer. Do so in a courteous manner.

9

▶ Smile during your interview. It will make a difference in how your voice sounds.

▶ Never interrupt the interviewer.

▶ Accept silence. If you have sufficiently answered a question, silence is acceptable while the interviewer prepares for the next question. Do not fill the silence with meaningless chatter, but you might ask a question that is related to your last response.

▶ Avoid sneezing or coughing. If these are unavoidable, say "excuse me." Never yawn, chew gum, eat, or drink during an interview.

▶ Always say "thank you" at the end of the phone interview, indicate your interest, and ask when to expect further word regarding other possible interviews.

success steps

TELEPHONE INTERVIEW ETIQUETTE

1. Ensure that the contact information in your cover letter and resume is correct.

2. Have a professional-sounding message on your answering machine or voice mail.

3. Keep a list of companies you have contacted by the phone.

4. Prepare by researching the company and writing down questions.

5. Find a location where you will not be disturbed during the phone interview.

6. Take notes.

7. Courteously let the employer know if you cannot hear what he or she is saying.

8. Smile during your interview. Your voice will convey a pleasant demeanor.

9. Never interrupt the interviewer.

10. Accept silence. If you have sufficiently answered a question, allow the interviewer to prepare for the next question. You may ask a question related to your last response, but do not fill the silence with meaningless chatter.

11. Avoid sneezing or coughing. If these are unavoidable, say "excuse me."

12. At the end of the phone interview, say "thank you," indicate your interest, and ask when to expect word regarding other possible interviews.

9

apply it

Phone Interview Role-Play

GOAL: To demonstrate the ability to use good phone manners during a phone interview.

STEP 1: Form pairs with other students in your class.

STEP 2: With scenarios provided by the instructor, role-play a phone interview. One student will be the employer and the other student the job applicant. Treat the role-playing seriously, since this activity can help prepare you for real-life phone interviews. After the role-playing is accomplished, the student playing the employer should constructively critique the job applicant on his or her phone manners and phone interviewing abilities. Where could the job applicants improve? What did they do right? If needed, redo the role-playing so you can practice and improve on your phone interviewing abilities. Reverse roles to allow for each student to represent the employer and the job applicant.

STEP 3: Write a brief report on what you learned from this activity and consider putting this information in your Learning Portfolio.

▶ REFLECTION QUESTION

- Do you think you would do well in a phone interview? What areas might you be able to improve in order to be more effective in a phone interview?

❓ CRITICAL THINKING QUESTION

9–2. How would individuals with some hearing loss deal with potential phone interviews? How might technology assist in responding to this issue?

Interviews that take place over a meal require specific etiquette considerations and special attention to manners.

©Digital Vision

MEALTIME INTERVIEWS

Some employers may choose to have one of the interviews scheduled over breakfast, lunch, or dinner. If this occurs, consider the following:

▶ Do not choose the most expensive item on the menu. Even though the meal will be paid for by the employer, be reasonable with your selection.

▶ Choose an item on the menu that will not be messy. Avoid finger foods or items that can be sloppy, such as spaghetti and barbecued ribs.

▶ Avoid using black pepper. Pepper can get stuck in teeth.

▶ Use good table manners, such as placing the napkin in your lap prior to beginning the meal, keeping elbows off the table, and using the appropriate utensils.

▶ Never talk with your mouth full. Take small bites and swallow before answering a question.

▶ Use your napkin often to wipe your mouth.

9

▶ Do not order alcoholic beverages during an interview meal.

▶ After the meal, excuse yourself to go to the restroom. Check for food particles in teeth before returning to the table.

Further information regarding general table manners can be located on the Internet.

---

success steps

SUCCESSFUL MEALTIME INTERVIEWING

1. Do not choose the most expensive item on the menu.

2. Choose an item on the menu that will not be messy.

3. Avoid using pepper, as it can become stuck in your teeth.

4. Use good table manners. Place the napkin in your lap prior to beginning the meal, keep elbows off the table, and use the appropriate utensils.

5. Take small bites and swallow before answering a question. Never talk with your mouth full.

6. Keep your professional appearance by using your napkin to wipe your mouth frequently.

7. Do not order alcoholic beverages.

8. After the meal, excuse yourself to go to the restroom. Check for food particles in teeth before returning to the table.

---

apply it

Mealtime Interviewing

GOAL: *To develop a better understanding of how to effectively interview over a meal.*

STEP 1: Conduct research on the Internet and/or at the library regarding how to effectively interview over a meal.

STEP 2: Write a brief report regarding your findings.

STEP 3: Consider placing the report on Mealtime Interviewing in your Learning Portfolio.

9

CHAPTER SUMMARY

This chapter focused on acceptable etiquette in the job search process. The importance of etiquette cannot be overstated, as employers appreciate high standards of behavior. The manners that you demonstrate are not only appealing to an employer, but represent how you will treat clients in the future. In addition to emphasizing the importance of etiquette to your success in the job search and in the impression you make as a professional, general etiquette guidelines were provided. Then, etiquette requirements for specialized interview situations, including telephone and mealtime interviews, were reviewed.

POINTS TO KEEP IN MIND

In this chapter, several main points were discussed in detail:

▶ Employers seek technically qualified individuals who also demonstrate good manners.

▶ Demonstrating phone etiquette is an important element of the job search process.

▶ Phone interviews are just as important as in-person interviews and should be treated with as much care and attention.

▶ Interviews conducted on cell phones require specific etiquette and considerations.

▶ General table manners need to be followed during a mealtime interview.

LEARNING OBJECTIVES REVISITED

Review the learning objectives for this chapter and rate your level of achievement for each objective using the rating scale provided. For each objective on which you do not rate yourself as a 3, outline a plan of action that you will take to fully achieve the objective. Include a time frame for this plan.

1 = did not successfully achieve objective

2 = understand what is needed, but need more study or practice

3 = achieved learning objective thoroughly

9

	1	2	3
Explain the importance of utilizing proper etiquette during the job search.	☐	☐	☐
Discuss ways that job applicants can demonstrate good manners.	☐	☐	☐
Describe the issues that a job applicant should pay attention to when it comes to using a cell phone for an interview.	☐	☐	☐
Discuss standards associated with effective phone interviewing.	☐	☐	☐
Explain important considerations to make when an interview is conducted over a meal.	☐	☐	☐
Demonstrate the ability to use good phone manners during a phone interview.	☐	☐	☐

Steps to Achieve Unmet Objectives

Steps	Due Date
1. _____	_____
2. _____	_____
3. _____	_____
4. _____	_____

SUGGESTED ITEMS FOR LEARNING PORTFOLIO

▶ Importance of Proper Etiquette: This activity will familiarize you with the importance placed by employers on appropriate etiquette in the job search.

▶ Phone Interview Role-Play: This activity will give you an opportunity to practice telephone interview skills.

▶ Mealtime Interviewing: This activity will help you develop effective mealtime interview skills.

REFERENCES

Caroselli, M. (2000). Nine etiquette tips for job seekers. Retrieved April 6, 2005, from the Dow Jones Career Journal Web site: http://www .careerjournal.com/jobhunting/strategies/20000301-caroselli.html

Crawford Hentz, M. (n.d.(a)). Phone interview etiquette can propel you to the next step in the hiring process. Quintessential Careers. Retrieved April 6, 2005, from http://www.quintcareers.com/phone_interview_etiquette.html

Crawford Hentz, M. (n.d.(b)). Phone interviewing do's and don'ts. Quintessential Careers. Retrieved April 6, 2005, from http://www.quintcareers.com/phone_interviewing-dos-donts.html

9

©Digital Vision

CHAPTER OUTLINE

Rejection in the Job Search

Attitudes for Success

Getting Feedback

Self-Evaluation

Creating an Action Plan

10 Dealing with Rejection

THE BIG PICTURE

CHAPTER	
10	100%
9	90%
8	80%
7	70%
6	60%
5	50%
4	40%
3	30%
2	20%
1	10%

LEARNING OBJECTIVES

By the end of this chapter, you will achieve the following objectives:

▶ Describe attitudes that contribute to outcomes of job interviews.

▶ Describe constructive attitudes toward job rejection.

▶ Explain the purpose of getting feedback from the employer when denied a job.

▶ Describe methods of obtaining feedback from employers.

▶ Describe the process of self-evaluation for assessing interviewing skills.

▶ Develop a preliminary self-evaluation tool.

▶ Describe the steps in creating an action plan for improving job search skills.

● TOPIC SCENARIO

Matt Ferthstone graduated from his academic program three months ago and has been seeking employment ever since. To date, his responses have been a combination of first interviews and rejection letters without an interview, resulting in a high degree of frustration. Matt feels discouraged and concerned because he must find a job to pay off student loans as well as to meet general living expenses. He feels that the more he tries, the less success he has.

Based on Matt's situation, answer the following questions:

▶ What factors might be contributing to Matt's lack of success in obtaining employment?

▶ How might Matt's frustration contribute to his difficulty in getting hired?

▶ How can Matt keep a positive outlook?

▶ What are some methods Matt might use to assess his job search skills?

▶ What resources might Matt use to develop his skills?

● REJECTION IN THE JOB SEARCH

Although it is likely that no one enjoys rejection of any kind, being declined for a job or being denied an interview *is* a part of the job search process. Receiving a rejection letter can be a positive way to develop your skills and expand your opportunities. Having the proper mindset and using rejection as a way to learn about yourself and develop weak areas are significant aspects of approaching rejection with a positive attitude.

BEING DECLINED IS PART OF THE JOB SEARCH

Gordon (2003) reminds us that elimination from consideration for a position is a normal part of the job search. She emphasizes that the way you view not being hired is instrumental in continuing the job search with a positive attitude. Accepting that a certain amount of rejection is to be expected in your search will prepare you for the inevitable. You may feel disappointment, but you will be more likely to see being turned away from a job in its proper perspective.

SELF-REFLECTION IS CRITICAL

Having the ability to look at yourself and evaluate your strengths and weaknesses is an essential element of using rejection as a positive experience. Self-assessment will help you to look objectively at yourself and set appropriate goals for your development according to the demands of your field. You can use rejection as a vehicle for accomplishing this and moving closer to achieving your professional goals. Record your self-reflection and observations in a journal to review your responses as you conduct your search.

apply it

Job Search Journal

GOAL: To develop insight into your perspectives on the job search, maintain a positive mindset, and track the outcomes of your search.

STEP 1: Create a journal (hard copy or electronic) that you will use on a consistent basis throughout your job search. Select a format that is convenient and appealing to you and that you will use.

STEP 2: Record the events of your job search. Include both positive and disappointing incidents as well as your emotional reactions to each. Examine each reaction and make a judgment regarding whether it is a constructive response.

STEP 3: If your response is less than constructive, apply one of the techniques discussed in this chapter. Look for the opportunities that present themselves throughout your search and take note of them. Record your responses to the process, including changes in your perspective.

STEP 4: Note the actions that you choose to take based on your changed perspective. Compare these actions to those that you might have taken if you had a less positive mindset.

STEP 5: Note the outcomes of your positive actions.

STEP 6: Consider placing your journal entries in your Learning Portfolio.

©Image Source Limited

Although no one enjoys receiving a rejection letter for a desired position, being declined for a job can lead to other opportunities.

10

ATTITUDES FOR SUCCESS

In addition to developing effective interviewing skills and job search strategies, there are actions you can take to prepare yourself for rejection when it occurs. Remember that being declined for a percentage of positions or not being called for an interview is inevitable. Assuming the appropriate outlook on the job application process can put you in a healthier frame of mind. The following suggestions for preparing your perspective on possible rejection are adapted from Bensley (n.d.):

▶ **Remember that you are one of many applicants.** Employers can receive hundreds of resumes for one position. When one person is selected for the position, it does not mean that the remaining applicants were not qualified. It means that one qualified person was selected from many.

▶ **Don't build yourself up for a disappointment.** Maintain a neutral, yet positive and hopeful outlook on any employment prospect. View the position as a possibility, but balance that with tempered emotions.

▶ **Avoid the negative.** When you are anticipating something, it is often easy to become anxious and recall bad experiences or failures. Doing so may cause you to anticipate negative outcomes and behave in a manner that invites disappointment. Be careful not to anticipate negative outcomes that can exaggerate your fears. Chabon-Berger (n.d.) suggests recalling your successful achievements, identifying the feelings associated with them, and engaging in positive self-talk, telling yourself positive things about the situation.

▶ **Use visualization.** Visualization is the process of seeing yourself in the position you desire and is related to emphasizing the positive. Use visualization to minimize your fears and maximize the positive messages that you send to employers. A positive approach will not eliminate rejections but can contribute to a greater chance for success as well as improve your frame of mind. See humor in situations whenever possible.

▶ **Accept the rules.** As in any game, there are rules for job searching, and you may not like some of them. Still, the reality is that you perform certain aspects of the process in defined ways. There is sometimes a tendency to become aggravated and negative about elements that we don't like. Recognize the realities of the job search process and accept those that are not flexible.

10

success steps

ATTITUDES FOR SUCCESS

1. Remember that you are one of many applicants.
2. Don't build yourself up for a disappointment. Approach the job opportunity with a realistic perspective.
3. Do not be overly negative.
4. Use visualization to develop a positive attitude.
5. Accept and follow the rules.

REFLECTION QUESTIONS

- How do you typically respond to rejection or disappointment?
- Do you believe your response is negative or positive?
- How would you change your response?

CRITICAL THINKING QUESTIONS

10–1. What steps can you take to make your responses to rejection or disappointment more positive?
10–2. How would doing so contribute to your success in the job search process?

KEEPING A PERSPECTIVE ON REJECTION

Putting yourself in a healthy frame of mind can lessen the blow of learning you were not hired, but positive thinking will not entirely eliminate its occurrence. The manner in which you view a situation has significant impact on the way you feel about it, think about it, and respond. When you are declined for a position, carefully assess how you are thinking about the situation. Keep the following points in mind:

▶ **Rejection is not a reflection of your skills or worth.** Companies have numerous criteria for hiring, including specific needs, timing, and other factors of which you might not be aware. Reasons for your not being hired can be many and varied, none of which reflect on your professional talent (Gordon, 2003).

▶ **Being declined is a small piece of the bigger picture.** Gordon (2003) points out that the emotional impact of rejection is a short-term price to pay for the longer-term satisfaction of a rewarding career. Focus on the characteristics you are developing that will be valuable to you in the long term, such as self-confidence and the ability to communicate with many types of professionals.

▶ **There might be something better out there.** Dattani (2004) points out that rejections sometimes pave the way for greater success. Dattani gives the example of J. K. Rowling, author of the famed *Harry Potter* books, who was initially turned down by several publishers in Britain before her now-famous books were accepted for publication. Another example that Dattani cites is film director Steven Spielberg, who was refused admission to the University of Southern California because of a low grade-point average. If you don't get your first choice now, know that there might be something better waiting for you.

10

? CRITICAL THINKING QUESTION

10–3. What other methods can you think of that would contribute to maintaining a positive perspective?

Following up with an employer or interviewer even after rejection can put you in a positive light and may open the door to additional opportunity. Make note of feedback so that you can incorporate it into your professional presentation.

Look for opportunities and what you can learn. As with many adverse situations, opportunity can grow from rejection. There is much to be learned from rejection, including insights about your presentation, skills you need to develop, and improved interviewing skills. The next section of this chapter explores techniques for seeing opportunity in rejection and using the experience.

success steps

KEEPING A PERSPECTIVE ON REJECTION

1. Rejection is not a reflection of your skills or worth.
2. Being declined is a small piece of the bigger picture.
3. There might be something better out there.
4. Look for opportunities and what you can learn.

GETTING FEEDBACK

Once you have adopted a healthy perspective on being declined for a job or not getting an interview, you are ready to make the best of the situation by learning as much as you can from the experience. Opportunities include gaining insight into your interviewing proficiency, learning where your technical skills can be improved, and increasing your chances for expanded networking. Consider the following possibilities for learning from rejection:

Apply what you have learned. There is much to be learned in the job-seeking and interviewing process. Being required to interact with other professionals, market your expertise, and use effective communication are just some of the skills you will practice during the job search. Paying attention to the effectiveness of these skills can provide insight into how you can polish and develop your professional presentation. Even if you are denied a position, use the experience to evaluate and improve your skills.

Follow up with the interviewer or contact person. Indiana University School of Law Career Services (n.d.) emphasizes the importance of following up a rejection letter with an acknowledgment. Although this sounds counterintuitive, sending a note can lay the

©Image Source Limited

10

foundation for future opportunity. Reasons for sending a brief yet sincere note include the following:

▶ You will stand out from the crowd. Very few people write thank-you notes following interviews, especially in situations where they have been rejected for employment opportunities. A note of acknowledgment is likely to be remembered.

▶ You may be offered another chance. There are situations in which the applicant who is accepted for the job doesn't work out or changes his or her mind after being made an offer. Your acknowledgment note just might make you stand out enough that you will be considered in place of the other candidate.

▶ You may be considered for another position if one is available.

Job-Employment-Guide (2004–2005) suggests that the follow-up letter contain the following elements:

▶ appreciation for letting you know the results, even though you are disappointed at not getting the position

▶ appreciation for the time, effort, and thoughtfulness given to you by interviewers

▶ appreciation for the opportunity to get to know the organization and its people, and what impressed you about it

▶ a statement of your continued interest in the organization

▶ a request to contact you if another suitable position becomes available or if the status of the current position changes

▶ **Use rejection as an opportunity to learn.** Being declined for a position can be a valuable learning experience. It is appropriate and effective to contact the interviewer and request feedback regarding why you were not considered for the position. Express appreciation for the interviewer's assistance during the interview process, as well as your disappointment in not being selected. Explain that you are interested in developing and improving your skills, and feedback would be helpful. Specifically, ask for feedback on skills that you might develop, ways that you might improve your resume, and other information that would be helpful to you in your situation. Respond to any feedback professionally and with an open mind. Thank the individual for his or her time, honesty, and assistance.

▶ **Apply feedback to your professional development.** Use the feedback that you receive to assess your skills, improve the quality of your resume, and enhance your job search strategies. Seriously and thoughtfully consider how you might incorporate the feedback into your professional plan. Set goals and identify strategies for meeting

10

them. For example, if you receive the feedback that you seemed to lack knowledge about certain aspects of your field, determine what you need to learn, identify resources for doing so, and set a plan in place for completing your goal by a specific date. The final section of this chapter will focus on self-evaluation and assessment of your career strategies.

> REFLECTION QUESTIONS

- Have you ever turned a disappointment into an opportunity?
- Recall the circumstances. What did you think about in order to see the opportunity? What action did you take?

? CRITICAL THINKING QUESTION

10–4. What other techniques might you use to turn disappointment into an opportunity?

---

success steps

CREATING OPPORTUNITY FROM REJECTION

1. Apply what you have learned.
2. Follow up with the interviewer or contact person.
3. Use rejection as an opportunity to learn.
4. Apply feedback to your professional development.

---

apply it

Asking for Feedback

GOAL: To increase your comfort and skills in requesting feedback after being declined for a position.

STEP 1: Form small groups of four students each. Two students will be the interviewers and two the job applicants.

STEP 2: Allow several minutes for the interviewers to write a script for giving feedback to the job applicants and for the applicants to prepare to ask for feedback. Note that it may be more difficult for the applicants to prepare because, as it would be in reality, they will not know what feedback they are going to receive. Applicants should prepare in a general way.

STEP 3: Role-play the scenarios that you have created. The pair of students not role-playing should observe and provide feedback following the role-plays.

STEP 4: Change roles and repeat the process.

STEP 5: Determine how you will incorporate the feedback that you receive into your interviewing and job search activities.

STEP 6: Consider placing your script and notes of the feedback that you receive in your Learning Portfolio.

Your Name
Your Address
City, State, Zip Code
Date

Interviewer's Name
Name of Organization
Address
City, State, Zip Code

Dear Mr. or Ms. _____:

Thank you for your follow-up letter regarding the computer programming position at XYZ Corporation. Although I was disappointed at not being considered for the position, I do appreciate your getting back to me, as well as the time and consideration given to me by the XYZ staff.

I very much enjoyed meeting you and _____ (insert names of other individuals you met during the interview process). I was especially impressed with the new computer systems you are developing, which clearly demonstrates XYZ's commitment to leadership in technology.

I remain interested in contributing my skills to your organization. Please feel free to contact me if a position suited to my qualifications becomes available or if the status of the programming position changes.

Thank you again for your time and assistance.

Sincerely,

Your Name

An effective follow-up letter after being declined for a job will express appreciation for the interviewer's time, state positive impressions of the organization, and reiterate your interest in the company.

SELF-EVALUATION

Self-evaluation requires reflection and an honest appraisal of your strengths and weaknesses. Evaluate each area of your performance and determine where you can improve. Set specific goals and dates for their completion. The following suggestions for evaluating and developing your job search process have been adapted from Cardillo (2005) and Indiana University School of Law Career Services (n.d.):

▶ **Assess your resume.** Evaluate your resume for spelling and grammatical errors. Ensure that it is concise, yet contains detailed, relevant information. Make sure that your resume clearly

10

summarizes your accomplishments and their results. Your resume should be printed on high-quality paper and printed in a 12-point font. Refer to Chapter 5 for details on preparing an effective resume. Assess your resume against accepted standards.

▶ **Examine your goals.** Review your goals and ensure that they are realistic for your level of training and experience. Consider that you may need to take a lower-level position to start. Be sure to also assess how well you are articulating how your skills apply to the needs of the employer. Consider your transferable skills. Are you demonstrating how transferable skills apply to the position? Evaluate your goals to make sure that your skills support them.

▶ **Get firsthand feedback.** In addition to seeking the feedback of interviewers and contacts at the job site, obtain input from a trusted source in your field, such as a friend or colleague, former instructor, or an internship supervisor. The individual should be someone that you trust and who can be honest with you.

▶ **Assess your self-presentation.** Your self-presentation includes all of your personal attributes perceived by a potential employer. Your appearance, the attitude that you project, your verbal and nonverbal communication, your ability to respond professionally and effectively to questions, and your general politeness and courtesy all contribute to how you present yourself to interviewers. This is also an area in which you may wish to seek feedback from a trusted source.

▶ **Re-evaluate your job-hunting methods.** Remember the importance of networking and getting your name and credentials in front of potential employers. Cardillo (2005) suggests sending your resume to organizations that are not necessarily advertising open positions, using professional recruiters, and developing your ability to market your skills. If you are using only one search method, such as print media or the Internet, expanding your techniques may be effective.

success steps

STEPS FOR SELF-EVALUATION

1. Assess your resume.

2. Examine your goals

3. Get firsthand feedback.

4. Assess your self-presentation.

5. Re-evaluate your job-hunting methods.

10

apply it

Internet Research

GOAL: To develop a resource bank for your job search.

STEP 1: Select an aspect of your job search about which you would like additional information. For example, you may need additional resources for developing interviewing skills. Conduct an Internet search using that aspect of the job search as your search term.

STEP 2: Create an electronic or hard copy file of resources that you find and to which you may refer throughout the job search process.

STEP 3: Repeat this process for other job search elements of interest.

STEP 4: Consider placing references to resources that you find in your Learning Portfolio.

? CRITICAL THINKING QUESTIONS

10–5. What other elements of the job search process might you evaluate?

10–6. From what other sources might you get effective feedback?

©Digital Vision

An effective self-evaluation often involves contacting professional colleagues and personal acquaintances to get a variety of feedback. Incorporate relevant feedback into your action plan.

CREATING AN ACTION PLAN

Any assessment of your skills that you complete will not be beneficial to you without follow-up. Successfully addressing issues that you discover in the evaluation process requires a sound plan and time-limited goals. The following steps are critical for effectively addressing concerns that you discover in the self-evaluation process:

▶ **Keep a written record.** A written record of your goals and the actions that you take will show you your accomplishments, motivate you, and let you know what you need to do.

▶ **Set goals.** Set goals based on your findings. Goals should be specific, measurable, and time limited. An example of a goal that meets these criteria is, "I will locate three Internet sources for resume writing by Friday." An example of a goal that does not meet these criteria is, "I will find some ideas for writing resumes." Making your goals specific, measurable, and time limited helps you complete them in a timely manner and lets you know if you have met criteria that will help you improve your job search.

▶ **Identify your resources.** List individuals, organizations, or sources such as the library and Internet that could serve as potential resources. Consider the career center at your school, as some schools offer certain services to their graduates. Other resources include

10

professional career counselors and agencies, although you should be aware that there may be a fee for these types of services.

▶ **Create a plan.** Review your resources and determine how they can best help you to achieve your goals. Once you have identified the resources that will support you in reaching your goals, it is important to create a plan that will allow you to succeed. Record your plan in writing and include the following information in your plan:

  ▶ **Break your goal into smaller objectives.** Identify small short-term tasks that will lead to your long-term goal. For example, if your self-assessment indicates the need to revise your resume, list the specific tasks you need to accomplish to revise the resume, such as placing greater focus on accomplishments, making the resume more concise, and printing the resume on a higher grade of paper.

  ▶ **Match your resources to your objectives.** Compare your resources to your objectives. Write specific steps to take that will allow you to complete each objective. For example, if you need to increase the focus of your resume on your accomplishments, look through your resources to determine methods for doing so. Based on your resources, list the changes you will make to each section of your resume. Seek additional resources if necessary.

  ▶ **Organize your steps in a logical sequence.** Determine the most logical order to complete the steps you have identified. Treat these steps as small goals by recording them in writing and ensuring that they are specific, measurable, and time limited.

  ▶ **Implement your steps.** Carry out your steps according to your plan and time frames. Adjust the timeline as needed. For example, if you are revising your resume and are called for an interview before your final completion date, you may decide to move your deadlines up so that your resume is updated prior to the interview.

▶ **Evaluate the changes you have made.** The self-assessment process is an ongoing procedure to ensure the continued quality of your job search efforts. Evaluate your changes to ensure that they are an improvement. Continue to make changes as necessary.

10

success steps

CREATING AN ACTION PLAN

1. Keep a written record.

2. Set goals. Identify your resources.

3. Create a plan.
   a. Break your goal into smaller objectives.
   b. Match your resources to your objectives.
   c. Organize your steps in a logical sequence.
   d. Implement your steps.
4. Evaluate the changes you have made.

apply it

An Evaluation Tool

GOAL: To develop a framework for evaluating job search strategies.

STEP 1: Create a table (hard copy or electronic) to use as a rubric for evaluating your job search methods. In the left-hand column of the table, list the elements to assess. Use the evaluation elements listed in this chapter and add others that are important to your situation. Across the top row of the table, list sources from which you will seek feedback (for example, colleagues, instructors, or interviewers).

STEP 2: Record the feedback on each element in the cell that corresponds to the type of feedback and the source. For example, if you get feedback on your resume from someone with whom you have interviewed, find the cell in the table that corresponds to those headings and record the feedback in the appropriate cell.

STEP 3: Review the completed rubric and use the information to establish your action plan.

STEP 4: Use an additional copy of the rubric to evaluate changes that you make to your job search strategies.

STEP 5: Consider placing completed evaluation rubrics in your Learning Portfolio.

> **REFLECTION QUESTIONS**
>
> - When have you used an action plan?
> - How did it affect the outcome of the task?

> **CRITICAL THINKING QUESTIONS**
>
> 10–7. If you have used an action plan, how might you change your approach to make the process more efficient?
> 10–8. If you have not used an action plan, how could an action plan improve your task performance?

CHAPTER SUMMARY

This chapter explored job rejection as an expected part of the job search. First, self-reflection is essential for understanding your reaction to rejection. Second, mindset was discussed as a critical part of approaching rejection in a positive way. You were encouraged to keep a positive perspective on rejection and to use it as a learning experience. The basis for doing this is to see the possibilities in rejection and to take advantage of opportunity. You learned steps for obtaining feedback from interviewers and from that, setting goals to develop weak areas. You learned steps for goal setting and creating an action plan to achieve your objectives.

POINTS TO KEEP IN MIND

In this chapter, several main points were discussed in detail:

- Recognize that rejection is a normal part of the job search.
- It is important to develop strong self-reflection skills so you can learn from the job search and be able to view rejection as a positive experience.
- Preparing your mindset and keeping a perspective on rejection can help keep you in a positive frame of mind.
- Rejection during the job search can be turned into an opportunity.
- It is important to evaluate your job search techniques by assessing your resume, examining your goals, getting firsthand feedback, and assessing your job search techniques.
- It is important to create an action plan that allows you to implement improvements identified in your self-evaluation.
- An action plan includes breaking your goals into steps, using your resources to carry out your steps, and creating a timeline for completion of the steps.
- Your job search should be a process of continual improvement and professional development.

LEARNING OBJECTIVES REVISITED

Review the learning objectives for this chapter and rate your level of achievement for each objective using the rating scale provided. For each objective on which you do not rate yourself as a 3, outline a plan of action that you will take to fully achieve the objective. Include a time frame for this plan.

1 = did not successfully achieve objective

2 = understand what is needed, but need more study or practice

3 = achieved learning objective thoroughly

	1	2	3
Describe attitudes that contribute to outcomes of job interviews.	☐	☐	☐
Describe constructive attitudes toward job rejection.	☐	☐	☐
Explain the purpose of getting feedback from the employer when declined a job.	☐	☐	☐
Describe methods of obtaining feedback from employers.	☐	☐	☐
Describe the process of self-evaluation for assessing interviewing skills.	☐	☐	☐
Develop a preliminary self-evaluation tool.	☐	☐	☐
Describe the steps in creating an action plan for improving job search skills.	☐	☐	☐

Steps to Achieve Unmet Objectives

Steps   Due Date

1. _____   _____

2. _____   _____

3. _____   _____

4. _____   _____

SUGGESTED ITEMS FOR LEARNING PORTFOLIO

▶ Reflection Questions and Answers

▶ Job Search Journal: This activity is designed to help you develop insight into your job search attitudes and strategies.

▶ Asking for Feedback: The purpose of this activity is to develop your ability to ask for feedback following being declined a position.

▶ Internet Research: Use this activity to develop a bank of resources to use during your job search.

▶ An Evaluation Tool: This activity is intended to help you develop a frame of reference for evaluating the effectiveness of your job search strategies.

10

REFERENCES

Bensley, R. L. (n.d.). Dealing with rejection in the job search. Placement and Career Services, New Mexico State University. Retrieved June 2, 2006, from http://placementmanual.com/workplace/workplace-08.html

Cardillo, D. (2005). Job-hunting challenges take some troubleshooting. Cardillo & Associates. Retrieved April 14, 2005, from http://www.dcardillo.com/articles/job-hunt.html

Chabon-Berger, T. (n.d.). Rejection doesn't have to be a dirty word: Slam the brakes on disappointment with these tips [Electronic version]. *The Palm Beach Post.* Retrieved April 14, 2005, from http://www.palmbeachclassifieds.com/employment/jobs/main/jobs112803_main.html

Dattani, M. (2004). Dealing with rejection. ivillage.co.uk. Retrieved June 2, 2006, from http://www.ivillage.co.uk/workcareer/survive/persondev/articles/0,,156471_661149,00.html

Gordon, J. (2003). Top 10 ways to deal with job rejection. Retrieved April 14, 2005, from http://www.qualitycoaching.com/Articles/rejection.html

Indiana University School of Law–Bloomington, Career Services. (n.d.). Your guide to successful interviewing: Follow up. Retrieved April 14, 2005, from http://www.law.indiana.edu/careers/guides/interview_followup.shtml

Job-Employment-Guide (2004–2005). Responding to employment rejection letter. Retrieved June 20, 2006, from http://www.job-employment-guide.com/employment-rejection-letter.html

10

Conclusion

MOVING ON FROM HERE

You are now familiar with the many elements of a successful job search. You should come away from the *100% Job Search Success* experience with ideas and strategies for showcasing your abilities and skills and for presenting yourself as a confident and competent professional.

The most important part of learning is application. Remember to keep the concepts and ideas that you have learned in reading this book at the top of your mind so that you can readily apply them to your job search and interviews. Practice interviewing with classmates, friends, and family members. Put time and effort into preparing your portfolio and getting ready to respond to questions commonly asked in interviews. Learn from each experience. Once you become employed, the next book in the *100% Success* series, *100% Career Success,* will support you in developing strategies for professional development and success as an employee.

You have received a strong overview of the skills needed for a successful job search. Seek additional information that will add to your success. Use the references provided for each chapter, and pursue additional resources according to your interests and needs.

Congratulations on your successes to date. May you have all the best as you pursue your goals.

Index

A

Abilities, 5
Action plan, 187–189
Appraisal review schedules, 152
Artifacts, 45, 49, 51–54
Assessment
    of organizations, 149–150
    portfolio, 47, 49, 52, 53
    self-assessment, 28–30, 188
Attitudes for success, 180–182

B

Background checks, 19
Barrett, H. C., 46, 47, 49
Barthel, B., 92, 93
Benefits, 46, 155
Bensley, R. L., 180
Bjorseth, 63
Body language, 166
Bonuses, sign-on, 152
Bowman, C. B., 132
Business cards, 137

C

Cardillo, D., 185, 186
Career portfolio, 47–49, 51–52, 53
Career services offices, 16, 33
Caroselli, M., 127, 165
Cell phone interviews, 169–171
Certification
    boards, 18–19
    requirements, 6–7
Chabon-Berger, T., 180
Chronological organization of
    portfolio, 55

Chronological resume, 85–86, 92
Communication
    electronic, 19
    practices, 9
Company, assessing, 149–150
Continuing education, 7, 18
Correspondence
    cover letters, 97–99
    other, 99
    thank-you letters, 76, 140,
        141, 167
Counselors, job, 16
Courtesies. See Etiquette
Cover letters, 97–99
Crawford Hentz, M., 168, 169
Criminal background checks, 19
Crosby, O., 75
Cultural network, 8–9
Culture
    defined, 8
    professional, 8–11
Current and updated, staying, 17–19
Curriculum vitae (CV), 89. See also
        Resume
CV (curriculum vitae), 89
Cyber-safety, 96

D

Dattani, M., 181
Deal, T. E., 8, 11
Developmental portfolio, 46–47, 49,
    52, 53
Dikel, M. F., 90, 96
Dikel, M. R., 29
Directories, of companies, 149
Dressing for success, 106–121

body type, 110–112
confidence and, 110
dress standards, 8
first impressions, 109
grooming considerations,
    113–114
interview dressing, 76,
    112–118
particulars of, 110–112
professional wardrobe,
    118–119

E

Electronic communication, 19
Electronic portfolio, 49–50
Elevator speech, 73–74
Ethics, professional, 10–11
Etiquette, 162–176
    importance of, 164–165
    job search, 165–167
    mealtime interviews, 171–172
    phone interviews, 168–171
    special situations, 168–172
Evaluation
    evaluation tool, 189
    self-evaluation, 185–187, 188
Experience
    gaining, 27, 30–38
    internship and, 31–38
    requirements, 6

F

Faculty, as informational
    resources, 16
Feedback, 182–185, 186
Flantzer, H., 63, 65

Follow-up
    action plan, 187–189
    interview, 140–141, 182–185
Functional organization of
        portfolio, 54
Functional resume, 86–87

G

Goals, 26–28, 187
    examination of, 186
    setting, 26–28, 185, 187
Goldrick-Jones, A., 92, 93
Gordon, J., 178, 181
Government sources, 14

H

Hansen, R. S., 33, 131, 135,
        153, 154
Hess, P. M., 91
History of profession, 12
Hoover, Myrna, 148, 151, 152

I

Industry and job research, 2–23
    industry requirements, 6–8
    professional culture, 8–11
    professional socialization,
        11–13
    sources for, 13–17
    staying current and updated,
        17–19
    understanding your
        industry, 4–11
Industry requirements, 6–8
Informational interview, 15–16,
        75–77
Information sources, reliable, 11
Interests
    interest inventories, 29
    understanding your own, 4–5
Internet
    as informational resource, 13–14
    safety on, 96
    Web forums and e-mail lists, 19
    Web resumes, 90, 95–96

Internship, 31–38
    locating the best, 33–35
    purpose of, 31–33
    success in, 35–38
Interpersonal relationships, 8–9
Interpersonal skills, 28
Interviews, 122–145. See also
        Negotiation
    addressing weaknesses,
        139–140
    cell phone, 169–171
    dressing for, 76, 112–118
    feedback from, 182–184
    follow-up, 140–141,
        182–185
    handling, 135–140
    informational, 15–16, 75–77
    mealtime, 171–172
    nervousness and, 132–133
    nonverbal behaviors and,
        133–135
    phone, 168–171
    portfolio and, 45
    preparing for, 124–130, 166
    questions, 127–130
    tactics, successful, 130–140

J

Job counselors, 16
Job description, 125–126
Job offer, 149–155. See also
        Negotiation
    accepting or declining,
        158–159
    assessing the organization,
        149–150
    benefits package, 155
    job location and relocation
        benefits, 151
    negotiable factors, 151
    salary, 152–154, 157–158
    sign-on bonuses, 152
    start date, 151
    understanding the job, 150
Job research, 2–23. See also Industry
        and job research

K

Kelly, S., 155
Kennedy, A. A., 8, 11
Kovar, R., 62, 63
Kurow, D., 63, 71, 73

L

Larson, B., 113
Learning portfolio, 46–47, 49,
        52, 53
Libraries, as informational
        resources, 17
Licensure boards, 18–19
Location of job, 151
Lumsden, J., 50, 54

M

Machowski, D. A., 158
Mulligan, B., 128

N

Negotiation, 146–161. See also
        Job offer
    accepting or declining a job offer,
        158–159
    appraisal review schedules, 152
    assessing the organization,
        149–150
    benefits package, 155
    do's and don'ts, 155–158
    job location and relocation
        benefits, 151
    job offer, assessing and
        negotiating, 149–155
    negotiable factors, 151
    purpose of, 148–149
    salary, 152–154, 157–158
    sign-on bonuses, 152
    start date, 151
    understanding the job, 150
Networking and self-promotion, 15,
        60–81
    defined, 15, 62
    described, 63–64
    elevator speech, 73–74

informational interview, 75–77
purpose of, 65
steps, 67–73
tips/guidelines for, 64, 70–71
venues, 65–67
Newberger, N., 114
Nonverbal behaviors, 133–135

O

Organization, assessing,
    149–150

P

Pages, M., 110
Personality tests, 29
Personality, understanding, 6
Phone interviews, 168–171
Pillsbury, Ceil, 131
Pitney, W. A., 11
Plan, action, 187–189
Politeness. *See* Etiquette
Portfolio, 42–59
    artifacts for, 45, 49, 51–54
    assessment, 47, 49, 52, 53
    chronological organization, 55
    combination format, 50
    contents of, 50–51, 53
    electronic, 49–50
    evaluation of, 55–56
    formats, 49–50
    functional organization, 54
    hard copy, 50
    learning or developmental,
        46–47, 49, 52, 53
    organization of, 54–55
    professional/career, 47–49,
        51–52, 53
    purposes of, 44–46
    types of, 46–49
Professional authority, 9–10
Professional culture, 8–11
Professional organizations
    informational research and,
        14–15
    joining, 12

staying current and updated
    through, 17–19
Professional portfolio, 47–49,
    51–52, 53
Professional publications, 18
Professional socialization, 11–13
Professional standards, 12, 37
Professional values and ethics,
    10–11
Promotion. *See* Networking and
    self-promotion

R

Recommendations, 99–101
Record, written, 187
References and recommendations,
    99–101
Rejection, 176–192
    action plan and, 187–189
    attitudes for success, 180–182
    feedback and, 182–185, 186
    in job search, 178–179
    keeping perspective on, 181–182
    as an opportunity, 182–184
    as part of job search, 178–179
    self-evaluation and, 185–187
    self-reflection and, 179
Relocation benefits, 151
Requirements, professional/industry,
    6–8
Research. *See* Industry and
    job research
Resources
    for industry research, 13–14
    job search, 16, 187–188
Resume, 82–105
    assessment of, 185–186
    chronological, 85–86, 92
    combination, 88
    cover letters and, 97–99
    curriculum vitae (CV), 89
    electronic, 89–90
    e-mail, 89–90, 94–95
    formats, 89–90
    functional, 86–87
    guidelines to creating, 90–94

other correspondence and, 99
purpose of, 84–85
references and recommendations,
    99–101
types of, 85–89, 91
using technology to send, 94–97
Web, 90, 95–96
Role models, 12
Rowling, J. K., 181

S

Salary, 152–154, 157–158
Self-assessment, 28–30, 188
Self-evaluation, 185–187, 188
Self-presentation, 186
Self-promotion. *See* Networking
    and self-promotion
Self-reflection, 179
Shalaway, L., 50, 51
Sign-on bonuses, 152
Simmons, A., 50, 54
Skills, 24–41
    assessing and developing, 24–41
    gaining, 30–38
    goals and, 26–28
    internship and, 31–38
    interpersonal, 28
    inventories, 29
    self-assessment, 28–30
    soft, 28
    technical, 28
    transferable, 8, 28
Socialization, professional, 11–13
Soft skills, 28, 47
Spielberg, Steven, 181
Springfield, E., 46, 47, 48
Standards, professional, 12, 37
Success, attitudes for, 180–182

T

Technical skills, 28
Telephone interviews, 168–171
Teschendorf, B., 11
Thank-you letters, 76, 140, 141, 167
Timeliness, 165–166
Transferable skills, 8, 28

U

Updated, staying current and, 17–19

V

Values
  professional, 10–11
  understanding your own, 5–6
Visualization, 180

W

Wardrobe. *See* Dressing for success
Web
  forums and e-mail lists, 19
  resumes on, 90, 95–96
  safety on, 96

Weinstein, B., 140
Welch, T., 63, 70
World Wide Web. *See* Web

Z

Zucker, R., 71